Dealing with Trusts & Consequential Liens from the Courts of Heaven

Finding Freedom from the Storms of Life

Volume 2 of the Bonds & Trusts Series

By

Dr. Ron M. Horner

Dealing with Trusts & Consequential Liens from the Courts of Heaven

Finding Freedom from the Storms of Life

Volume 2 of the Bonds & Trusts Series

By
Dr. Ron M. Horner

LifeSpring International Ministries
PO Box 5847
Pinehurst, North Carolina 28374
RonHorner.com

Dealing with Trusts & Consequential Liens from the Courts of Heaven
Finding Freedom from the Storms of Life

Copyright © 2022 Dr. Ron M. Horner

Scripture is taken from the New King James Version®. Copyright © 1982 by Thomas Nelson. Used by permission. All rights reserved. (Unless otherwise noted.)

Scripture quotations marked (KJV) are from the King James Version of the Bible.

Scripture quotations marked (TPT) are from The Passion Translation®, Copyright © 2017, 2018 by BroadStreet Publishing Group, LLC. Used by permission. All rights reserved. ThePassionTranslation.com

Scripture marked (THE MIRROR) is taken from The Mirror Study Bible by Francois du Toit. Copyright © 2021 All Rights Reserved. Used by permission of The Author.

Any trademarks mentioned are the property of their respective owners.

All rights reserved. This book is protected by the copyright laws of the United States of America. This book may not be copied or reprinted for commercial gain or profit. The use of short quotations or occasional page copying for personal, or group study is permitted and encouraged. Permission will be granted upon request.

Requests for bulk sales discounts, editorial permissions, or other information should be addressed to:

LifeSpring Publishing
PO Box 5847
Pinehurst, NC 28374 USA

Additional copies available at www.courtsofheaven.net

ISBN 13 TP: 978-1-953684-23-3
ISBN 13 eBook: 978-1-953684-22-6

Cover Design by Dr. Ron M. Horner with Darian Horner Design (www.darianhorner.com)
Image: 123rf.com, # 55745326

First Edition: May 2022

10 9 8 7 6 5 4 3 2 1

Printed in the United States of America

Table of Contents

Acknowledgements...i
Preface..iii
Chapter 1 Understanding Trusts.. 1
Chapter 2 The Trust Registry... 15
Chapter 3 Requesting Godly Trusts
  & Removing Ungodly Trusts.. 25
Chapter 4 Consequential Liens 31
Chapter 5 Constructive Trusts... 55
Chapter 6 Wisdom's House 65
Chapter 7 Red & Black Capture Bags 69
Chapter 8 Silver & Gold Capture Bags 75
Chapter 9 Purple Capture Bags 93
Chapter 10 Green, Blue & Grey Capture Bags 97
Chapter 11 Orange, Brown & Tan Capture Bags 109
Chapter 12 Pink Capture Bags.. 127
Chapter 13 Rough Places in the Road 139
Chapter 14 Unweaving Domains 145
Chapter 15 The Banners of the Lord.............................. 153
Chapter 16 Malcolm's Instruction................................... 165
Chapter 17 The Treatise of Trust.................................... 177

Chapter 18 The Hall of Commerce 193

Chapter 19 Court of Trade 203

Chapter 20 Becoming a Living Rainbow 209

Chapter 21 Conclusion 219

Appendix A 221

Extended Trusts Listing 221

The Trust Registry 229

Step-by-Step Procedure 231

Capture Bag Colors & Their Meaning 233

Multiplication 235

Multiplication, Part II 241

Division 247

Scriptures of Trusts 251

Works Cited 255

Description 257

About the Author 259

Other Books by Dr. Ron M. Horner 261

Acknowledgements

In February of 2022, Heaven began unveiling this revelation to me and Stephanie Shearin, my Executive Assistant. I honor her for her humble service to the King. Thank you, Stephanie.

My additional thanks go to CeCe Compton and Joyce Ruck Poupart for their additions to the listings of Godly and Ungodly Trusts as well as their other contributions, and to Anna Horan and Fran Wipf for their editorial assistance. Thank you, ladies.

Preface

A couple of years ago, Heaven released to us the revelation regarding the Bond Registry. This information is within my book titled *Releasing Bonds from the Courts of Heaven*, and it has been life changing for many. If have not yet read the material in that book, I would recommend you do so before reading this sequel. An understanding of bonds and the bond registry will aid you greatly in understanding the revelation contained in this book.

As a quick refresher, a bond is a legal instrument in the spiritual realm that causes actions or reactions in the physical realm. Bonds can be Godly or ungodly, and their effect on your life can be either positive or negative, depending on their origin. The enemy uses ungodly bonds to make our lives more difficult than they are intended to be. Heaven instructed us on how to remove ungodly bonds and replace them with Godly bonds that will work to align our lives with the plans and purposes of Heaven instead of darkness. The practice of this revelation in our ministry has produced much freedom.

Heaven has now downloaded to us the next level of this revelation and it allows us to continue to find even greater levels of freedom, faster. It is the principle of spiritual trusts. In simple terms, a trust is a framework that holds an inheritance for someone. In the natural realm, we are familiar with the idea that a parent may wish to leave a significant sum for their children to inherit, but they will often put that sum into a trust that ensures there are certain protections in place before the child can access the funds—for example, the child might need to be 21 years old. There exists cause and effect relationship to access the trust—if 'this' happens, then 'this' can be released.

In similar fashion, our Heavenly Father has provided inheritance in a series of trusts for each of His children, and our eyes have recently been opened to the numerous examples of Godly inheritances held in trust that are laid out in Scripture. These will be detailed later in this book.

The enemy, a prolific copy-cat, has instituted his own system of evil trusts, in order to pass along an ungodly inheritance based on sin and iniquity to each generation, or to block us from receiving the Godly inheritance that is rightfully ours.

We are excited that Heaven has opened our eyes to this new understanding. In this book, we share conversations with Heaven that describe the process by which we can eliminate the ungodly trusts and thus remove the painful inheritance from our lives. At the same time, we can institute processes to access more of the Godly inheritance that is promised to us in Scripture as sons of the Most High God.

There are some new terms and tools to be aware of before we jump into Heaven's instructions.

Parameters—each type of trust has 'parameters' which are essentially barricades the enemy has erected to prevent someone from accessing their inheritance. Think of someone building a fence to keep you out of your own house. That is a picture of how parameters work. Later in this book we will show you how to demolish the parameters that are preventing you from receiving your full inheritance in Christ.

Consequential liens—Every action or inaction on our part creates a cause-and-effect situation in our lives. Consequential liens are legal tools that result from our actions or inactions. When Adam and Eve ate the apple, the enemy placed a consequential lien on all of humanity and he suddenly had a legal right to impact mankind in negative ways that he did not have before. The consequences of their sin gave him legal access to us by way of a consequential lien.

Constructive trusts—A constructive trust originates from the Father to benefit mankind. Its purpose is to dismantle the powers of darkness in order to empower, restore, and release the Glory of the Lord.

Capturing angels—A specific type of angel who can be commissioned to capture and destroy the work of the enemy.

Capture bags—Tools used by capturing angels to apprehend evil devices in the spirit realm. They are different colors and different sizes depending on the work at hand.

We also make mention of several different characters who assist us to unpack this revelation, including:

Stephanie—Executive Assistant to Dr. Ron Horner

Lydia—a woman in white linen who often teaches and advises us from Heaven

Malcolm—a man in white linen who often teaches and advises us from Heaven

Ezekiel—the angel over LifeSpring International Ministries

Following is a simple outline for dealing with ungodly trusts. It will be explained in more detail later in the book. It is a step-by-step process that is already producing tremendous freedom in our clients and team members as we put these understandings into practice.

Step-by-Step

- Open the Bond Registry to the Personal page
- Bring the tab forward (You will know there is an ungodly trust)[1]

---

[1] You will see or sense something like a Post It note sticking out of the edge of the Personal page on the person's Bond Registry. Take hold of this tab and move it to the forefront. It is the record of the ungodly trust.

- Find the parameters around the ungodly trust
- Repent as necessary
- Strike the parameters
- Capture the princes—the dominion
- Freedom will come

The issue of trusts is an entirely new concept to us, but one that will result in tremendous freedom for those whose lives have been a constant storm where they have not been able to gain freedom. Freedom *IS* available! You are about to see it manifest in your life. Hang on! You are in for an exciting ride!

Chapter 1
Understanding Trusts

I first heard mention of the concept of Trusts in a short paragraph by Ruthie Andrews on her Facebook page. It intrigued me so I sought out more information from Heaven on the subject. A few weeks later, Heaven obliged as Stephanie (my Executive Assistant) and I engaged Heaven to be taught by Malcolm.

Stephanie and I had accessed the Business Complex of Heaven specifically to learn about the concept of Trusts. Although we had some natural understanding of the legal agreements known as Trusts of various types, we had little understanding of heavenly Trusts and so we accessed Heaven for answers. There are Godly trusts and ungodly trusts. We were about to learn much more.

We took a seat in the classroom where we had been taken and Malcolm, who often advises and teaches us in our ministry was present to teach us. He began, "There are bondages that look like trusts, that sound like trusts, that even feel like trusts in the natural. These bondages prevent explorations in Heaven, Kingdom Dynamics of Heaven, Throne Room entries of Heaven, and even the simplicities of income. These bondages prevent people from interacting with Heaven, from developing a relationship with their Father to the fullest extent. from receiving in both the supernatural and natural arenas as Heaven intends. These are bondages. It is a parameter or (fence) that the enemy has put around someone's access into the aforementioned places."

Stephanie noted, "I'm seeing it as in other times, other realms, and other dimensions—in time and out of time. That is how it is structured in the kingdom of darkness."

Malcolm continued, "They take what would be the goods of Heaven, the access, the entrances, the gifts, the knowledge, and even portals, and hijack them using evil timelines, using the spirit of fear in people's lives, using spiritual droughts because of the spirit of religion in people's lives, and using bitterness and unforgiveness. This is how these things are taken into a form of captivity that is like a trust—with various parameters outlining why someone is unable to access the things that are the Kingdom of Heaven, and that Heaven has made available to the sons and daughters.

"These are strategies of Hell, not unlike what you have read about in Aprile Osborne's book on the boardroom work of forces of hell. The Kingdom of Heaven can easily gain this back on behalf of the peoples. Some will be gained back through fasting. Most will be through the paradigms of prayer and the courtroom work. This is like what you already know about the dynamics of the Court of Cancellations. The cancellation of these parameters is done through repentance work for coming into agreement with the spirit of fear, for embracing doubt, for embracing the spirit of religion, all of which you have been taught to break. This work will be done through the Court of Cancellations."

Stephanie had to pause to explain that her soul had suddenly become very excited because, as Malcolm was talking, diagrams were going up on the whiteboard.

We asked, "What are identifiers of trusts?"

Malcolm replied, "When you have clients/people who are unable to obtain breakthrough in their everyday waking lives of freedoms that they know are theirs, you are likely looking at an ungodly trust, or a Godly trust that has had ungodly parameters placed against it. It is one more point of access through the Courts of Heaven for freedom. It will be in one of your books, Ron, just like all the other bondages. This is easily handled in the Court of Cancellations because of Jesus and because of his love for the peoples. This is part of the provision. This is part of the finished work."

We inquired, "Will it show up in the registry as well if we are looking for it?"

He replied, "If you're looking for it. Create another parameter in the courtroom work being done by the advocates to look in the Registry for the ungodly parameters of a Trust."

Stephanie interjected, "I immediately saw the simplicity of how we do work in the courts. I saw someone going to the Mercy Court where there had been unforgiveness, doubt, or partnering with the spirit of religion—and repenting for such. They go to the Court of Cancellations of any oaths or covenants and then to the Court of Titles and Deeds, requesting that the title deeds returned to Jesus, and also severing the spirit of religion." Malcolm explained, "The Senior Advocates have access to that prayer paradigm. When they see this come up, this is a prayer that they can have that person in front of them pray against the spirit of religion that will break off the parameters. There are some that come to us that need that specifically done. This will open a floodgate where there are no longer conditions or limitations to their freedoms, their access, their gifts, or their incomes."

"Is this an extra layer of freedom, Malcolm?" We asked.

"No," he replied, "this is an extra *tool* for freedom."

"Are there different kinds of trusts? In the natural we have different kinds?" I asked.

Malcolm responded by drawing a diagram on the whiteboard at the front of the classroom. He drew a giant parenthesis ( ) and immediately Stephanie heard the word '(parameter).' He said, "All of it is in inside of those parentheses. It is *all encompassing.* That is the simplicity of Heaven."

He said, "We already know that some find the Courtrooms of Heaven daunting. This is not daunting work. We are not making it more complicated. You just didn't know anything about it. This is just part of the tools in the tool set. There will be more coming down the pike."

With that, Malcolm laid down his chalk.

Let's Practice

Immediately I wanted to put this into practice. We asked for access to the Court of Records. I wanted us to look at my Guest Registry knowing that if any trusts were impacting me, I would be able to discover it in the Guest Registry.[2]

Court of Records

I told Stephanie, "We are looking to see if there are any trusts." I remembered from an engagement a few months ago we were told that when viewing the Guest Registry, that if you were not looking for a particular

---

[2] More is explained later in this chapter in the section "The Trust Registry."

thing you may not see it in the Guest Registry (even though it may be in it).

Stephanie began, "I would like access into the Court of Records, please. I would like to see Dr. Ron's personal records regarding trusts."

She was handed a Manila folder whereupon she asked that an angel or an attendant would help her to read what was in the folder properly on behalf of Dr. Ron and for the Kingdom of Heaven.

She opened the folder and began to read, "I see what looks like a lien in the parentheses, which is a parameter as a part of this trust."

"Can you tell me more?" She asked.

The attendant said, "The enemy has put a lien on the open doors of the trust that the Kingdom of Heaven has for you."

Stephanie asked, "Why is there a lien?"

He replied, "Well, we're teaching you that there can be liens put upon a trust as well."

Stephanie said to me, "I'll tell you how I saw it. As soon as I opened it up, in the parentheses are what would have looked like parameters, it had the word 'lien' and it the word was *leaning* as if it were against a wall."

I said, "Well, they want you to get the message."

Stephanie replied, "I got it."

I asked, "Is this something we deal with in the Court of Titles and Deeds or is this a Court Cancellations situation?"

We were told, "Cancellations. All parameters of trusts will be in the Court of Cancellations. Then they said, "You know the lien is easily satisfied by the blood of Jesus. Right?"

Continuing, I said, "Well, Father, we request access to the Court of Cancellations."

"Is there any repentance involved?" I asked.

"This one was illegally done," was the reply. When something was illegally done like in this case, no repentance is generally required. You can move ahead to the next step.

"Father, I'm requesting that the lien placed upon me via the trust, by the enemy against the open doors that the Kingdom of Heaven has for me, I request it be completely removed from me."

Stephanie described what she was seeing, "I'm seeing the parameter with the word 'lien' in the middle of it being washed with living water mixed with blood and it is collapsing under the movement of the water and the blood."

The attendant said, "In this instance, movement is like a frequency. Movement *is* as a frequency."

Stephanie asked, "Is this satisfied?"

"It is," we were told. "They just wanted us to see how it worked."

Continuing, Stephanie asked, "Is there anything else we need to do at this point related to this one? Any commissioning of angels or anything of this sort?"

"Yes," we were told. "In this teaching to the advocates[3] and to the peoples, commission the angels to go and remove the evil parameters because we all have trusts that Heaven wants to be available to us. Realize the enemy is the one that puts the parameters in place to hinder your trusts from being fulfilled. Commission the angels to remove the parameters that the enemy has placed on the heavenly trust. Then, commission them to strike the parameters."[4]

Stephanie suddenly saw it as in a document that you strike something like a ~~word~~. That is what that word means. In this instance, they are to strike the parameters.

Envision it like this:

(Spiritual blindness) is the ungodly parameter within parentheses. Follow the instructions given above and commission the angels to STRIKE the parameter, that is, remove it from the books. The ungodly parameter of (spiritual blindness) becomes ( ).

---

[3] Referring to our Senior and Junior Advocates who lead our Personal Advocacy Sessions.
[4] To "strike the parameters" is akin to the legal jargon of "striking from the record" which means to remove it as if it had never been on the record.

I asked Malcolm, who had come near, "Did I hear you say that Heaven has Trusts on us?"

Godly Trusts

Malcolm responded in the affirmative. He then explained, "The enemy comes to interfere with us and our Trusts. When we are born, trusts are one of the things that the enemy can see. It is a part of the Kingdom Dynamics, and they are very specifically upon us and upon our DNA. The Trust that Heaven has given us has multiple meanings to it.

That trust is open access to the Father and all the Kingdom Dynamics that were mentioned before.

The enemy comes in to put parameters on that, to keep us from walking in the fullness of His Kingdom."

I asked, "Malcolm, can you give me a few parameters that hit the mark?"

He continued, "**Corruption.** Sin in general is corruption. Discuss the simplicity of sin. He said you are just going to be discussing the simplicity of what we know is sin. *Hamartia*, the Greek word commonly translated as sin means to miss the mark so as to forfeit the prize. Paul indicated his determination not to miss the mark. In Philippians 3:14 we read:

I press toward the mark for the prize of the high calling of God in Christ Jesus.

"Paul was determined to reach for the high call of God.

"The second parameter is **deviousness**. You will see this in plain sight.

"Third parameter is **egregiousness** which is flagrant behavior (or shall I say 'misbehavior'). It is conduct that is in your face, because there is no fear of God.

"Fourth, **Satanism**. Everything that is Satanism or the world of Satanism—witchcraft, idolatry goes along with that. These are parameters that you will see."

Stephanie described what she was seeing, "As soon as I saw the visual of closing the parameters, right before that, and I saw what we would view as a manifestation of demonic presence, we deal with it, and then proceed to the closing of the parameters. The striking and the closing of the parameters stops that."

She said, "I'm trying to ascertain the one, two, three of how this is going to work."

He replied, "Remember this is just a tool."

Stephanie continued, "As you're doing this teaching here, he showed me that as you lead this corporately and talk about the parameters and the closing of them, and that the simplicity of the prayers and the Court of Cancellations, we will begin to hear and see demonic manifestations. We will take authority over it, call the angels to quiet them. Then there will be words of wisdom.

"We are to be invoking Wisdom to be in the middle of it every time where wisdom gives us the understanding—words of knowledge, of what that parameter—that specific parameter in that person is to strike and to close.

"Remember this is in time and out of time. When you close the parameters, do this in time and out of time. That is the instruction for the angels."

Malcolm said, "The list is as according to plan. Commission the angels to strike the parameters in time and out of time."

I began, "In the name of Jesus, I call Ezekiel near, his commanders, and his ranks; I call Stephanie's angels near, and we commission you to strike the parameters in time and out of time that the enemy has placed on the Trusts that the Lord has granted to us so that we can fulfill the purpose and destiny of God in fullness and all the Kingdom Dynamics that the Father wants us to walk in."

Malcolm said, "Kingdom Dynamics is the next thing we are going to learn about. There is a whole lot of stuff in that."

I then asked, "What else is in that folder?"

Stephanie turned the page and laughed when she saw the phrase, "Kingdom Dynamics." She flipped to the next page, but it was blank. (As of this writing we have not had the training Malcolm foretold, but I expect it to occur very soon.)

Putting it Into Practice

I told Stephanie, "Now let's do something as an exercise. Let's ask to look at my registry."

I said, "You want to sort by 'Trusts' and then 'Parameters on those Trusts.' For example, you should see that the lien that just got satisfied should be marked that it has been satisfied, or it should have a notation beside it."

Stephanie mused, "What my question right now is, what is that Trust's name?"

I heard, "Proverbs 3:5-6 '**Trust** in the LORD with all your heart, and lean not on your own understanding and in all your ways acknowledge Him and He will direct your paths.' There is a play on words where we call it. 'Trust in the Lord,' but He is making it a legal document.

Notice the wording of
'trust in the Lord with all your heart.'
It is a permission slip to trust the Lord
with all your heart.

"You already have that as part of your DNA to be able to do that. Religion has tried to stop that. Fear has tried to stifle it. All the junk that has happened in our life is just to keep us from trusting with *all* our heart, but that is the trust. If there is any lien against that trust, we can get that canceled in the Court of Cancellations.

"Look at the rest of that passage. If we trust with *ALL* our heart AND do not lean on our own understanding. We do not live under a lien on our ability to trust Him. If we will acknowledge Him in all our ways, we have a promise—He will direct (straighten or make right) our paths.

"We can look and see what other things that are 'Trusts' *of* the Lord. There are other verses that say, 'trust in the Lord.' Look in Psalms (and Proverbs) and you will find other things that are types of trusts."

Stephanie said, "I see you looking up the words 'trust.' like you originally looked up the words related to the Courts of Heaven. I have seen several names."

——— · ———

Chapter 2
The Trust Registry

Malcolm began to unpack some of the types of trusts that we have and experience. As the list unfolded, we realized that it contained arenas of trust that the Lord was looking at in our lives. Was it cleared, or did it contain something we needed to look at? We began to look at the list and the first thing on it was:

- **Trust of trust**—where people trust you. The original design of the Father was that you live life without suspicion. We were designed for trust, but the enemy has interfered. Now we have the parameter of (distrust)—the word in the parenthesis.

The next on the list was:

- **Trust as a father**—not as your daughters see you, but as people see *you* as a father figure.

Additional trusts could be Trust as a Mother or in Trust as a Nurturer.

As we looked at my list, this one was marked 'Cleared.' It had that as a notation.

Below the trust as a father is:

- **Trust as a son/daughter**—that's you and your relationship with the Father.

These are how we are to teach people to look in similar order to how we view the Bond Registry's Personal page, et cetera. This is how we are to view this. People can go in and look at this Trust Registry. People want a simplistic understanding of what the next step is. This is step-by-step, so next there is:

- **Trust as Income**—and under that are categories of:
    - **work**—the Father has created us with unique abilities and skill sets that are designed to be rewarded by others. You have a particular ability to do a certain thing, you find that thing and are employed for it. As a result, you sow time and effort, and the reward is financial provision. The better you are at what you do, the more you are rewarded. We are told that if you want to eat, you must work.[5]

---

[5] 2 Thessalonians 3:10

- **stewardship**—which includes tithes, offerings, first fruits, etc.

  We have to evaluate where we stand in regard to this aspect of trust. We have been taught (mostly by religion) not to trust the Father as provider. We have been taught that the Father cannot be depended upon. This is a lie. The fact that you have experienced provision in the past prophesies that you will have provision in the future.

  Do we trust His provision for us? Do we trust him that we will survive if we dedicate 10% of our income to Him as a tithe. The tithe is a barometer of trust in the arena of finances. Offerings is the next level of trust in that arena, followed by first fruits, and alms. All are levels of trust that we develop with the Father, the provider of all.

The next one is the:

- **Trust as a Friend**—under that is a category of:
  - **a friend that sticks closer than a brother**—to be that to someone on that level requires a level of trust and a willingness to live in forgiveness.

  And then,

- **a friend to all**—I see that as just the Kingdom Dynamics of being good to everybody, being a nice guy or nice lady.

  We typically don't see relationships as issues of trust, but really, they are *all about* trust. You cannot have a relationship without trust. The moment you stop trusting the other party, the relationship suffers. How are we doing in that arena?

Under that is the:

- **Trust of Ministry**—You are reading this book or listening to this teaching based on a level of trust that I will have something to say that benefits you and does not harm you. I hope to live up to that trust. We all have been harmed by those in leadership in the church. Some did the harm maliciously, but most probably did not. You have experienced deep wounds. I, too, have been wounded.

  However, the Trust of Ministry arena has multiple sides to it. The subcategories Malcolm pointed out are:

  - **Trust of Platform**—Do you trust the person on the platform? When the person on the platform violates that trust, will we forgive them as we have been forgiven, or will we allow that situation to taint our view of others in the ministry? Will we allow it to bleed over in not trusting God, who called that person to ministry?

- **Trust of Prayer**—Wrapped up in the Trust of Ministry is the question we have to ask ourselves. Do we trust prayer? Many have been disappointed when they did not see the desired result of something they may have prayed for over a long period of time. Some have found relief and a new measure of hope in the Courts of Heaven paradigm, but it is not an answer in all things. It is a set of tools that we can utilize to invite Heaven into our situations. Still, some have been disappointed in this paradigm as well. We must remember, prayer is not a vending machine where I put a certain phrase or phrases into the slot and out comes the answer. Prayer is the invitation to Heaven into your situation.

- **Trust of Seed**—Immediately when I saw 'seed,' it took me directly to the teaching we heard from Amanda Winder[6] and the word 'seed' was in gold. However, one of the implications of the Trust of Seed reflects to the Parable of the Sower in Mark 4. Jesus pointed out that in that parable, the seed

---

[6] See the blog post: https://amandawinder.com/2022/01/20/multiplication-part-ii/

was the Word of God, so the question is, "How are we doing in our trust of the Word of God?"

Many of us aren't doing too well in that category. We read our Bible, but it isn't alive to us. It is stories on a page. If it is stories on a page, then something needs to be fixed in the trust arena. Malcolm explained, "Well, you've just been taught what that means from Amanda [Winder]."[7]

- **Trust of Kings**—this involved the ability to trust the office a person stands in spiritually and otherwise.

The list continued:

- **Trust of Family**—There are three categories, your:
  - **Biological Family**—Do we trust our mom and dad, or our siblings? Our grandparents and cousins, uncles, and aunts? Many have had biological family that violated trust with us, and this is a difficult area to reconcile, but Heaven needs us to look again and will help us to forgive the violators and find healing and restoration. We must forgive as we have been forgiven. Paul instructed us in Ephesians 4:32: *And*

---

[7] See the two blog posts by Amanda Winder in the Appendix. Amanda is one of our Team Members.

be kind to one another, tenderhearted, forgiving one another, even as God in Christ forgave you.

Heaven wants all parties to be living out of their original design, not out of their brokenness.

The second category of family is:

- **Close Friends**—Those that are close like a brother. It goes up to that one under Trust as a Friend that says, 'a friend that sticks closer than a brother.'

The other one under family is the:

- **Family of God**—this is your literal brothers and sisters in Christ. Are we walking in love with them? Are we willing to offer a degree of trust to them and even if they mess up, forgive them? These are hard questions sometimes because wounds from a friend, from a brother or sister in the faith, are often tough pills to swallow. If you have experienced traumatic things as a result of trusting a brother or sister in Christ, are you willing to trust again?

The division created by violations of trust are simply to make an example of us to the world. Will we take the bait?

This is basically a Trust Registry and what we have been describing is your Personal page on your Trust Registry. But realize that because this is your Personal page, this Personal page affects all the other pages.

Malcolm inquired, "Do you remember the phrase 'co-laboring?'"

I answered, "Yes."

Malcolm explained, "Co-labor in your own self as well. All these things work tangibly together."

Stephanie said, "I'm seeing the word vulnerability. As people are coming to know you and this ministry related to false accusations and parameters, the enemy would try to take one of those accusations to try to put parameters around this office, this legislative office, under the Trust of trust. The enemy would try to put parameters so there would be loss of trust towards you, the ministry personally, about the Courts of Heaven, about CourtsNet, about Sandhills Ecclesia, and the other facets of the ministry. I think that's why it is the one at the top, because it's the most vulnerable."

The aim of the enemy in this is so there develops a hardness of heart in you, so that you don't trust other people.

We realized this is a revelation, not unlike the bond revelation. Stephanie said, "I saw it being used like the way we review a Bond Registry. It has the same usefulness, and it has the same ability to disclose parameters. We have more to learn, but this was a wonderful start for us."

Malcolm added, "As part of the message many have lost trust and faith in Father God, because of the different trusts that have parameters inside of them from the enemy. As these parameters are eliminated by a strike, the trust between their heavenly Father and themselves will be reignited. They will be able to understand the indepthness of it, through the format you are releasing.

Trusting the Father is something many struggle with.

"The striking of the parameters will reignite the levels of love and heavenly downloads from the Father. During this meeting it is an action item. It's an activation. This activation will be corporate, and you will move in this individually as you minister."

Chapter 3
Requesting Godly Trusts & Removing Ungodly Trusts

CeCe Compton, one of our intercessors sent information she had just received from Heaven just as we were finishing this book. It gave good insight concerning how we can utilize trust for others. Here is what she shared with me:

> *Trusts can be placed on others. Request them in the Court of Titles and Deeds. While they do not replace bonds they are needed and stronger than bonds. These will bring about greater protection, greater works, signs, wonders, and miracles. We can also request these be enforced in the Court of Enforcement.*

To use this in the Bond Registry, simply listen to Holy Spirit and ask for the Trusts that He directs be added to the appropriate page in their Bond Registry. You may need to request a Trust of the Father be granted to them.

Examples of Godly Trusts to Request

Trust of Above and Beyond	Trust of Angelic Assistance
Trust of Boldness	Trust of Clarity
Trust of Communion	Trust of Courage
Trust of Destiny	Trust of Deut. 11:24
Trust of Divine Health	Trust of Due Season
Trust of Father's Intent for Me	Trust of Father's Wisdom
Trust of Forgiveness	Trust of Friendship
Trust of Friendship	Trust of Honesty
Trust of Hope	Trust of In Time & Out of Time
Trust of Jesus' Blood	Trust of John 3:16
Trust of Knowledge	Trust of Love of Humankind
Trust of Loyalty	Trust of Luke 10:19
Trust of Mercy	Trust of Multiplication
Trust of My Scroll	Trust of Passive Income
Trust of Passover	Trust of Precious in His Sight
Trust of Prosperity	Trust of Provision
Trust of Reconciliation	Trust of Relationships

Trust of Restoration	Trust of Righteous Commerce
Trust of Safety	Trust of Salvation
Trust of Self-Control	Trust of Sonship
Trust of the Glory of God	Trust of the Goodness of God
Trust of the Supernatural	Trust of the Word of God
Trust of Trust	Trust of Truth
Trust of Value	Trust of Wholeness
Trust of Wisdom's Pearls	

(An extended list can be found in the Appendix.)

You can request these Godly Trusts be added in the Court of Titles and Deeds simply by requesting they be added to the appropriate page in their Bond Registry or Trust Registry. The one will populate the other. Heaven will take care of that detail.

Dealing with Ungodly Trusts

You have the option to see ungodly trusts on the Bond Registry as well as seeing them in the Trust Registry or even in a persons' Outstanding Folder. The important thing is to repent for the sin in the generations regarding the particular ungodly trust, and request access to the Court of Cancellations for the removal of the ungodly trust from the person's records. Request that the angels strike from the record the ungodly trust and see the trust stricken from their record.

Finish up by following the procedure outlined in the chapter on the constructive trusts on behalf of the person you are ministering to.

Examples of Ungodly Trusts to Remove

Trust of Addiction	Trust of Astrology
Trust of Auto-immune Disease	Trust of Cancer
Trust of Death	Trust of False Gods
Trust of Falsehood	Trust of Financial Ruin
Trust of Freemasonry	Trust of Gluttony
Trust of Human Wisdom	Trust of Idols
Trust of Intellect	Trust of Knowledge
Trust of Lying Signs & Wonders	Trust of Mammon
Trust of Mithraism	Trust in One's Strength
Trust of Pharmakeia	Trust of Profane Worship
Trust of Re-occurring Calamity	Trust of Seen

Trust of Self	Trust of Sorcery
Trust of Soul	Trust of Stagnation
Trust of Stolen Time	Trust of the Bastard
Trust of Witchcraft	Trust of Zodiac Signs

(An extended list can be found in the Appendix.)

Auto-Renew Clauses

Concerning many of the ungodly trusts, you need to be aware that many have an automatic renewal clause built into them. This means that although you cancel it today, it will automatically reset itself and reoccur. Sometimes this reset will occur outside of this dimension. To deal with this, access the Court of Cancellations and request the cancellation of every renewal clause built into these trusts in time and out of time and in every dimension and space in-between. That should have the desired effect of completely obliterating the ungodly trust and all of its parameters.

Chapter 4
Consequential Liens

Stephanie and I had requested more instruction from Malcolm. He wanted to give us *A Lesson in Liening*. Continuing from our lesson a couple of days before, he began, "Just as you saw the lien in the parentheses, we can discuss liens out of parentheses." Malcolm often used the word parameters instead of parentheses.

Stephanie asked, "Can you explain that to me?" She began to describe what she was seeing. "The picture I'm seeing first, the lien in parentheses, and now the lien out of the parentheses."

Malcolm continued, "They correlate. They can be combined. The liens that we know about already can be a combination lien. When you look in the Registry, you will see:

- liens within parameters which are set by the enemy (covered in the previous chapter) and,

- the ones outside the parameters which the enemy sets are of heavier weight. They both are enemy liens, but the ones outside the parameters have heavier weight—they are weightier.

(Malcolm had illustrated these using parentheses to encapsulate the ungodly parameter, i.e., spiritual blindness, deafness, hardness of heart, etc. and other liens that have no parenthesis surrounding them. These, he explained, are the weightier ones.)

Stephanie said, "My obvious question, Malcolm, is why did we learn about the non-weightier ones first?"

He replied, "You had to have a starting point. This is Heaven's design. The weightier liens carry a different frequency. They carry a stronger point of reference within them. But remember, they are just as easily handled by the Just Judge, our great Father—the one who loves us.

The weightier liens come more in the generational lines.

"They are stronger in the generational curses.

The lien is weightier because there are greater principalities attached to it, which brings greater demonic activity in a person's life.

"The weightier the lien, *the stronger the demonic presence*. As you are dealing with them you will see demonic manifestations, but they are easily overcome by the Blood of the Lamb."

Stephanie said to me, "As we work as advocates on these liens with people, there will be greater freedom from the deep, deep demonic strongholds in people's lives. The demonic manifestations of old will present, but the cancellation of the parameters of these liens in the Court of Cancellations will immediately dissipate the stronghold the demonic has and freedom will come immediately."

She began to describe what she was seeing, "This is like I'm standing in front of somebody. We are doing this work and there's an actual manifestation like we saw in the Bible—thrashing, throwing themselves around, that kind of thing. But the minute that this is done in the Court of Cancellations, it ends."

"Malcolm," Stephanie asked, "Is this different from the demonic guards with LHS's and how they present?"

He replied, "These are stronger principalities involved, but just as easily conquered. This is freedom. This is the wonder working power of Jesus's blood, the forgiveness of sins, and the cancellations of stronger liens within parameters in the court systems.

"There will be some, that'll be intimidated by this at first because of the manifestations, but stand in the knowledge that this is also courtroom work and there is nothing to fear because greater is He that is within you than he that is in the world."

Principalities are easily silenced as Kingdom people walk in the authority that is theirs.

Stephanie interjected, "He is showing me that we can call the angels to silence them when they begin to manifest."

Malcolm said, "You have some interesting work ahead of you."

Stephanie replied, "Yes, Malcolm, I would say so."

Malcolm continued, "It is a piece of the puzzle—a tool."

Stephanie said, "He is reminding me of that Scripture concerning what we are doing with people. They will have a sense of, 'There is no greater friendship than one that lays their life down for someone.' This is a type of laying down your life for someone in the work that we're doing, because it's not for our benefit, it is for their benefit. That is what is also going to draw people into this ministry more and more."

I asked, "How do we recognize this level of lien?"

Malcolm replied, "You will look in the Registry. Remember this is courtroom work the same as the Bond Registry. You are just looking at the next level—at the next column."

"What is this particular type of lien called?" I asked.

Malcolm replied, "A consequential lien. It is of greater consequence from the generational line.

"You have dealt with many of these consequences through the book on Mithraism and the Freemasonry book.[8] This will go along with those. This is another step. This is a separate tool, but an equally effective tool."

Stephanie described what she was seeing, "What he just showed me really quickly was the Mithraism and the Freemasonry book were the first steps and are still necessary and they still need to be done because of the overall work we're doing.

> *[19] The entire universe is standing on tiptoe, yearning to see the unveiling of God's glorious sons and daughters! [20]For against its will the universe itself has had to endure the empty futility resulting from the **consequences** of human sin. But now, with eager expectation. (Romans 8:19-20) (TPT) (Emphasis Mine)*

"This next thing is not something they are going to have to read, or know, or understand, but as advocates, it's one of the tools that will be used. Like when we are standing in a conference, we are going to see demonic manifestations. It will be taken care of just like that

---

[8] Referring to *Freedom from Mithraism* by Dr. Ron M. Horner and *Overcoming the False Verdicts of Freemasonry* by Dr. Ron M. Horner (LifeSpring Publishing).

through the Court of Cancellations and the cancellation of the parameter of this type of lien."

To clarify, I said, "We request the cancellation of this consequential lien in the Court of Cancellations—is that right, Malcolm?"

"Yes," he replied, "and the consequences and impact of them."

I noted, "Repentance also, as directed by Holy Spirit."

"Yes, as you break the generational curses off of people," he replied.

"Consequential liens are typically from generational lines, correct?" I asked.

"They are," he replied.

Continuing my clarification, I asked, "Are there consequential liens that are outside of a generational line?"

"Yes," he replied, "but they don't present themselves as these kinds of liens. They are the liens[9] you already know about."

Stephanie added, "The way I'm looking at this, Ron, the way that it is being presented to me is while we are doing so much bond work and as our Advocates have done so much bond work, that as they are going through

---

[9] The liens Malcolm was speaking about are not those we deal with in the Court of Titles & Deeds. The liens he is speaking of are dealt with in the Court of Cancellations.

a person's Bond Registry and they ask, 'Is there a consequential lien?' It will show as a tab between the personal and the family page of the Bond Registry. It must be taken care of in the Court of Cancellations.

A principality is attached to the consequential lien.

"The difference is there is a principality attached to the consequential lien—a stronger principality than what is coming with the parameter liens, right?"

Malcom replied, "Right. They carry a heavier weight because they have a principality attached to them."

Stephanie asked, "Malcolm, are you showing us that those that haven't done the Mithraism book and the Freemasonry book, that this is a freedom they can get right then and there? Is that what you're saying?"

Malcolm sat down with a book and when he opened the book in it, it said 'Principality' and there was language underneath it as a description or a definition.

"Yes," he replied. "The principality has taken a deeper root and those that have not read the Mithraism and the Freemasonry book, this is how you get past that, if someone hasn't done that type of work."

Describing what she was envisioning, Stephanie said, "It is as if we are standing in a conference and we are dealing with people, this is how it is playing out in front of me. People come that haven't read these books. We can't ask them to go home tonight and read the Freemasonry book and the Mithraism book and we will see you tomorrow. This is where there is freedom right in that moment. Is that right, Malcolm?"

He said, "Yes. The need for reading the Freemasonry and Mithraism book is still very important and a necessary part of the work of the Advocates with the clients. In all the other circumstances, this is the immediate work you can do about the consequential liens manifested by the principalities."

He began showing Stephanie what happens when someone is casting out a demon or dealing with a principality, and he said, "The church has believed, because of the Scripture that if you don't keep your house cleaned, they can come back seven times. That is why this consequential lien needs to be taken care of. The return of seven more cannot happen when the consequential lien is cancelled, and the generational ties are broken."

I asked, "Do we request the cancellation of the assignment of the principality?"

Stephanie asked, "Will you show us the steps?"

Malcolm replied, "The forgiveness of sin and the generational curses in the generational line *is* the removal of the principality and the cancellation of his assignment."

I asked, "Do we have angels that need to come and be involved?"

He said, "You can request angelic assistance to remove them."

Stephanie asked, "Malcolm, can you show me this in a picture?"

Procedure for Freedom

Describing what was before her, she said, "I'm seeing you, Dr. Ron, standing in front of a woman and she begins presenting a manifestation. You ask the Holy Spirit, 'Is there a consequential lien in this person's life?' And the Holy Spirit tells you, 'Yes.'

"You call the angels to come, and you repent on behalf of the generations and the consequential lien that was placed. The Court of Cancellations is invoked, you receive the righteous verdict, and the principality is removed. You request 'As if it never were,' request the blood of Jesus, and request the parameters to be closed.

"Well, like that! I saw them close."

I asked Malcolm, "Earlier, you referred to a combination? Malcolm, can you help us understand?"

Consequential Liens Described

In reply he said, "The correlation is of the liens themselves. There are two types of liens. They are both handled in the same court. Regular liens are the liens that come with the common sins of a person that are placed upon them from oaths, vows, and transactions. Regular liens do not have principalities—it is more like a tying of hands where one is unable to move forward because of the lien that is placed upon them.

And then there are the consequential liens. **The consequential lien has a principality attached** to it, causing greater conflict to be inflicted upon the person. That is why you will see manifestations when you uncover a consequential lien. As you do this work and you see a regular lien, always ask the question, 'Is there a consequential lien, as well?' This is the second step.

"We are quite capable with the first step of the regular liens. That is why this second step is being invoked now. It is the next step. It is the next tool—the next resource. It's simple. Ask for the understanding. If there's a regular lien,[10] take care of that in the Court of Titles and Deeds and then ask if there is a consequential lien and invoke the Court of Cancellations on that as well for complete freedom. Close the parameters."

I remarked, "This plays into the trusts we were talking about previously.

Stephanie noted, "This is going to bring in so much more freedom for people on a different level."

---

[10] A regular lien is explained more fully in my book *Engaging the Courts for Ownership and Order*, LifeSpring Publishing, 2018. The essence of a regular lien is that it can stop forward movement in one's life and must be satisfied by the blood of Jesus.

Another Way to Describe Them

One of our Junior Advocates describes how Heaven helped him grasp what consequential liens are:

At the Ft. Myers Conference, Dr. Ron was teaching on the newest revelation of consequential liens. I was feverishly taking notes trying to wrap my head around the concept. Suddenly Dr. Ron called the whole Courts of Heaven team of advocates to come forward and informed us we are going to apply what we just learned. I felt like a deer in headlights. I took a deep breath, a hard swallow (gulp), I quickly prayed 'Jesus, you have to help me do this,' and was ready to give it a go. I was paired up with Stephanie at first and a young lady was assigned to us. We asked for access to the Court of Records to see what consequential liens were causing the storms in her life. In the spirit, we saw an envelope being handed to us. In this envelope, I saw what looked like a page of the Bond Registry.

In the first column, I saw the word depression— this was the assignment that was against the individual's life. In the second column, I could also sense there was depression which was generational. I was able to see in the next column there was a principality of fear & anxiety assigned. As I was discerning this suddenly, I saw an image appear that looked much like the way a grammar school mathematics problem called 'order of operations or PEMDAS'[11] *had looked. In the math equation you may have a numerical representation as follows:*

$$(4x2)4x2$$

In the spirit the way the consequential lien appeared to me was:

(Depression) Depression

I knew the depression in parentheses was the part of the consequential lien the individual had against their life, and depression outside the parenthesis was on their generational line from their ancestors. To the right of the liens was another column where I was able to identify the principalities. The words on the registry corresponded to the equation I had seen in the courtroom. This equation appeared much like looking at a lit up red neon sign.

(Depression) Depression -> Fear & Anxiety

We had asked the individual that we were praying for at this moment if this resonated with her, and she confirmed what we were seeing was accurate to the storm she was experiencing in her life.

Stephanie and I dealt with the consequential liens in the Court of Cancellations. Upon calling the angels in to strike the parameters, I saw two

---

[11] PEMDAS (parenthesis, exponents, multiplication, division, addition, subtraction)

angels come into the courtroom with pickaxes. These two angels wound up and swung at the neon sign lien equation '(Depression) Depression.' Suddenly I saw the sign shatter like glass, the light went out and the words on the registry were struck through and then disappeared from the page. After this lady was set free, I was directed over to help another woman on my own. When I asked Heaven for her envelope of the consequential lien, she had one of grief that appeared like this: '(Grief) Grief—Death.' I was discerning there was a covenant with death tied to the grief. I had explained what I was seeing to the individual and asked if it resonated. She confirmed that she was in a period of sorrow and morning, and that many of the first born in her family line died prematurely. I could feel and see the physical manifestation of her sorrow.

We dealt with the consequential lien in the Court of Cancellations and requested the cancellation of the covenant with death over the family lines. We asked the angels to come, strike the parameters, and remove the principality. After concluding the court work, I felt the Holy Spirit pushing me to release the glory for her. Immediately, I could see her countenance had completely changed from sorrowful to content and even joyous. The Lord had restored her joy and was making her laugh just moments after dealing with the consequential lien. I was truly blessed to see how freedom was delivered instantly through these new concepts.

Ungodly Trusts

Malcolm was finished discussing this subject for today, so I had questions from our time together a couple of days before. I mentioned a session we had with a client the day prior, where I discovered an ungodly trust was involved. I wanted to know more.

I began by asking Malcolm, "Yesterday, in the session with our client, there was an ungodly trust involved, am I correct?"

"Yes, you are," he replied.

I asked, "Can you teach us a little bit about ungodly trusts?" To inform Stephanie of the situation with the client, I described that, in that case, there was an ancestor who entered into a trust agreement with darkness, and it had an automatic renewal clause; if someone tried to dissolve it, would automatically renew, and *it would renew in a different dimension.*

Malcolm replied saying, "That is why you close the parameters."

Stephanie remarked, "He is taking me back to that Scripture that we have all heard where if you sweep the house clean and they find seven more who come who are stronger. When you close the parameter, they can't come because they don't have that access anymore.

"Malcolm, can you give us a good definition of an ungodly trust?"

In response, Malcolm began writing on his board a step-by-step approach. He used the phrase "calm before the storm." Asking Malcolm for clarification, he responded to us with, "This is about storms in people's lives, and this is a storm in people's lives. They are seemingly in a constant storm. It is as if a storm will come and then dissipate. Then, the next storm comes, and they feel like they are in a constant storm. This is as a storm with the tossing to and fro."

I remarked, "These are earmarks of someone with an ungodly trust. They are always in a storm and are tossed to and fro and can never settle on anything. Would that be correct?"

A trust is designed to govern the access to an inheritance.[12]

Malcolm replied by showing a picture of billowing waves in a sea where a storm is present, and a little tiny ship is being tossed to and fro.

"That's the picture he's drawn for me," Stephanie noted.

He replied, "Yes. Those are the markers. What will present itself before you is what looks like a storm and a manifestation. But our Savior, the one who speaks to the storm has given you the authority to speak to the storm."

---

[12] This is one definition of a trust.

We asked about a friend's son who had been battling addiction issues. Would this apply to his situation we wondered. Were these ungodly parameters a part of his issue, we asked.

Malcolm showed Stephanie a picture of us closing the parameters of this addiction in his life and as she saw the parenthesis around the word (addiction), the word addiction disappeared and only the parentheses remained.

"What are some parameters, Malcolm?" we asked.

"Toxicity," he replied. "Toxicity is pollution from within."

I noted, "His (the friend's son's) brokenness makes him pollute himself continuously to medicate. Medicating himself is all he is doing."

Malcolm showed Stephanie a picture of a storm again, only this time, the storm was inside a person. She could see the storm inside of them in their belly. It is a pollution. It is a toxicity—because the principalities are polluted to their core."

We asked, "Can you explain the different parameters?"

He replied, "The parameter is the ungodly trust that the enemy has put on a person. It comes through generational sins and iniquities put in by a principality to its core. The dynamics of this are fluid, just like the waves—the tossing of the waves to and fro. They are fluid."

We asked, "Malcolm, are you saying that there are different reasons for these parameters or there are different parameters?"

He said, "It's inconsequential of the why. It just is. Generational sin encompasses all the things that you already know about. This is the closing—the finality, the closing of the consequences of the parameters. There was zero access that's allowed back in of these principalities that caused the tossing of the to and fro, and the turmoil and the pain.

"This is simple so keep it simple."

Stephanie said, "I just saw the word K-I-S-S."

Malcolm said, "Keep It Simple, Silly—not stupid."

The Gates of Hell

I commented, "Malcolm, the other day you began unpacking for us the trusts that the Father has in our behalf and how these parameters were impeding the fulfillment of that trust arrangement."

Malcolm began, "When the parameters are closed, the gates of hell cannot prevail against what the Father will release in a person's life: the freedoms that will come, the open doors, portals, gates, the blessings, the Father's love. It, too, is all encompassing. What He will pour out upon them, and in them, and through them, they will be able to receive. It is an unleashing of Heaven's gates and Glory on the person and their life. It's to them specific. It's not generational. It's to them specifically, for them, on behalf of them, because of His love for them. He will present himself in such a manner it will be undeniable."

Stephanie asked, "Are you saying it will be undeniable—that work of closing the parameters?"

"Yes," he replied. "It will become a relational thing in their life. The closing of those parameters will open wide the gates of the relationship the Father yearns for with the person, and they will be able to access it because the trust the enemy put on with the parameters and the consequences are no longer there."

"Proverbs 3:5-6 can be played out in someone's life. When it says, 'Trust in Lord with all your heart'— the ability to trust with all your heart is available as part of the Father's trust?" I asked.

"Yes," Malcolm replied. "That is the play on words here. That is why I told you from the beginning that this trust had multiple meanings. He is a good, good father. He desires this relationship. The Father has made the way for the relationship, but these parameters have been erected in their path."

Stephanie remarked, "I'm seeing it play out as like the Father being so overjoyed at this freedom, because He has provided the direct access, but there have been parameters put in place that have blocked this from that person being able to experience the Father. Once those ungodly parameters are removed, they are going to be able to experience Him now!"

Stephanie commented, "What keeps blowing my mind more and more, Dr. Ron, is the finished work of Jesus and all that really means. This is part of that."

"Yes," I replied. "Malcolm, Psalm 5:11 says, 'Let all those rejoice who put their trust in you, let them ever shout for joy because you defend them. Let those who love your name be joyful in you.' Those are trusts in our behalf for joy, and defense."

Malcolm replied, "Don't forget the trust that the gates of hell will not prevail, right?"

Stephanie asked, "Are you saying that when this parameter is done, the gates of hell cannot prevail anymore and there cannot be that consequential fault and parameter again?"

Malcolm replied:

Unless the person willingly opens themselves up to that parameter again, it is forever closed.

"Wow," was all that we could say.

I asked, "How can we accelerate this in the Father's sons' and daughters' lives?"

Malcolm said, "Knowledge is power. Tell them this—that there will be great rejoicing—shouting—when they realize the gates of hell cannot prevail, that this parameter is closed forever in their lives. The tossing to and fro is done."

At this point Stephanie could see how it would play out in a session with a client. She explained, "I would see Joyce in a session where after that consequential lien is dealt with, there will be words of knowledge given like a Godly bond, but they're not called Godly bonds. These are the open doors to Heaven. These are the gifts, the gates—all those things that will be available to that son or daughter. You're talking about words of knowledge—like what, Malcolm?"

I interjected, "For example, from that source I read in Psalm 5:11—joy, defense, and so on"

I asked Malcolm, "Are we on the right track?"

"Yes," he said. "As a matter of fact, you can use that and write that down. That's what it is—it is the Godly parameter."

Malcolm explained, "There was an original design for the Godly parameters and Satan has stolen once again what the parameters are supposed to be. Because in God's Kingdom, the Godly parameters are everything the King has that He gives His children. The enemy has put ungodly parameters to steal from Father's children because he hates God so much."

I continued, "I want to be simplistic to say that just like we have a Personal page, we also have a Family page, a Work/School/Ministry Page, and a Relationship page."

Malcolm added, "You can add this as a 'piece of a page' for the sake of seeing. These are not pages, as in the Bond Registry. It is one page. You can call this Generational."[13]

Stephanie explained, "We can look at the Family page as what's going on in our present tense family—things that are affecting our children and our parents. But this is the Generational page for those things not touched on in the Mithraism and the Freemasonry book.

"He just showed me how the devil is a liar and that there are other things that our generations came into agreement with or were a part of that allowed these principalities to become parameters down the generational line. He's showing me that in each individual person that that principality would present itself differently depending on the where the person lived, who they lived with, who their immediate friends and family were, so that principality through that generation would look and act differently in each person and manifest itself differently in each person. Whatever it is will still show up in their registry. That's part of the deception that was used."

I asked, "Is this simply like a column in the Bond Registry or is there a registry regarding page parameters?"

Stephanie began, "He's showing me a page that says Generations and in it is the parentheses (parameter) that

---

[13] See earlier in this chapter about the tab on the Bond Registry pages.

you asked to see. I'm not seeing more than one parameter. I'm only seeing one on that page—just one big one on the page.

"As I'm seeing this in my mind, as pictures, as a movie. I'm seeing the Personal page, then the person goes to the Family page. Then they go to the Business/Ministry page and then they go to the Relationship page. Are you showing me that we can go to the next page and it's Generational?"

Malcolm replied, "Generational should be the second page, although it is not necessarily a page. It's like a column, but you can turn from the Personal page and be right there at the Generational. Make sure that when you're done with that Personal page to look at the Generational parameters to see if there's a lien. That is the next step. The Generational page is essentially in between the Personal and Family pages because it is between generations. The generational line is between the person and their family. The generational line is in between those two things."

I added, "In a sense, there are five pages in that respect."

Malcolm replied, "Yes. But don't let the people be overwhelmed by five pages."

Stephanie continued, "I saw it like he turned the page and there was not all this stuff on the page. It just was one parameter. What we must know is as they move from that Personal page to this parameter to expect the manifestations. They are easily quieted."

I noted, "Kevin and Joyce have experienced that with some clients who would manifest as they went through the Bond Registry process. They didn't know how to obtain this degree of freedom."

Malcolm said, "This is not overwhelming, and this is not new, but this is new to you."

Again, Stephanie described what she was seeing. "I'm seeing lots and lots of movies in my head right now that are being played out, that Malcolm has given me—Holy Spirit has given me. With this revelation, when ministering to someone, we have an option. We can start with the Personal page of the Bond Registry and if we see a tab between the Personal page and the Family page, we know to deal with a consequential lien, or we can simply ask Holy Spirit, "Is there a consequential lien?"

I spoke up saying, "I have a question for you, Malcolm. You used the term consequential lien. Are we speaking of it being a result? Is it a consequence of actions and the generations?"

He replied, "Yes. consequential liens are specifically used by the enemy to steal the relational side with the Father. It put parameters around people to keep them from accessing the Father and cause them to have difficulty in the relationship with the Father, being unable to draw close, not trusting the Father, et cetera. They simply are **unable** to trust the Father."

Stephanie asked, "Are you saying Malcolm, this is going to break the barriers of people not trusting their earthly fathers, therefore, they cannot trust Father God?"

"Yes," he replied.

Stephanie continued, "Now he's showing me how earthly fathers wound their sons and daughters and empower that trust there. That is part of the parameter that is set in place in someone's life, where they are unable to have trust of the Heavenly Father because of the parameters put on them by the enemy on how they look at their earthly father. That is a huge issue with people, isn't it Malcolm?"

"Yes," he responded, "the levying of the parameters of this trust will in turn, allow the sons and daughters to fully trust their Heavenly Father."

Then he sat down. He laughed and said, "This is really easy (there is just a lot inside of it)." He showed me the words 'there's just a lot inside of it' in the parentheses as a funny, humorous joke.

As he was walking out, he said, "I give you ease."

We said, "Thank you, Malcolm. Thank you."

———·———

Chapter 5

Constructive Trusts

As our Senior Advocates began to implement the revelation of the consequential liens and trusts, more information began to be revealed. Joyce Ruck Poupart,[14] one of our Senior Advocates with a solid track record in helping advocate for people in the Courts of Heaven, received very interesting and powerful insight into what Heaven referred to as a constructive trust.

Here is what she wrote to me:

On Sunday, February 27, 2022, as I stepped into Heaven, I sensed I needed to look in the Outstanding Folder as there were things that were trying to hinder the ministry. I specifically was led to access the Court of Records and was impressed that there was an outstanding ungodly trust in place causing division.

---

[14] Joyce is a retired lawyer.

I dealt with it through the Court of Cancellations, as we had been taught.

The trust created blinders over the group, in terms of a mindset, and had become a blanket of strife on them. This had to be removed along with consequential liens which served as parameters.

I requested that the angels come in with all necessary bags—brown for principalities and powers, dominions and territories that had been established, black for witchcraft, red for infiltration, orange for domains, and blue for accusations.

The definition she received from the Father was:

A constructive trust involves a trade from Heaven of the highest order. It is not like a bond from man to God, but a constructive trust comes from God to man. It is from the Father. It becomes a domain, collapsing the frequency and foundation of the former trusts, liens, and consequential liens. It is a trade of My Word, My power, and the Anointing of My Spirit which trumps what Satan and his emissaries have done. It becomes an establishing platform to pray from. It is not only a trade and exchange from Heaven, but my [Constructive] Trust works and thereby 'empowers, restores, and dismantles' the powers of darkness. It is a bridge to cross over, filling the gap between what the demonic realm created and the portal of My Glory.

Wiktionary.com's definition of a constructive trust is:

A trust created by a court (regardless of the intent of the parties) to benefit a party that has been wrongfully deprived of its rights.[15]

As Joyce was praying for LifeSpring, she heard Father say, "Receive the Trust now for them and for yourselves. Establish the 'Trust of Unity.'"

She prayed:

Father, I request access to the Court of Records to request a constructive trust, a platform established by Heaven according to Psalm 11:3 which says: 'If the foundations be destroyed, what can the righteous do?'

Then she heard, "Replace My Word, My Grace, the trust being the foundation of God's Word, a measure of His grace." She continued her prayer:

Father, I request the following constructive trusts:

- *Constructive Trust of Unity*
- *Constructive Trust of Racial Harmony & Freedom*
- *Constructive Trust of Brotherhood and Sisterhood in Christ*
- *Constructive Trust of One race, one blood*
- *Constructive Trust for Divine Pathways to be Restored*

---

[15] https://duckduckgo.com/?t=ffab&q=constructive+trust+definition &ia=definition

- *Constructive Trust of Harvest Returned for the Body of Christ & LifeSpring International Ministries*
- *Constructive Trust of Comfort of the Brethren one to another*
- *Constructive Trust Communion and fellowship in the Holy Spirit, Amen.*

Joyce said, "I immediately saw the paperwork being prepared."

She continued, "I asked the Lord where the Trusts were to be established and He said, 'Ask Me,' so I did. I was led to request constructive trusts for the following:

- *Dr. Ron and staff*
- *Those attached or connected to the LifeSpring International Ministries*
- *The Body of Christ*
- *Those who will listen to LifeSpring.*

"I could see a white blanket which reminded me of the dominion Stephanie spoke about." Joyce directed:

I receive the constructive trust now in Jesus' name.

"Psalm 37:4 came to mind which says, 'Delight yourself also in the LORD, And He shall give you the desires of your heart.'

"I requested the assistance of the angels of the Trust Department to administer the constructive trust, like a sheet or platform to the realms involved, completely, accurately, securely, and firmly."

She concluded, "I then thanked the Lord for what was received."

This was the understanding Joyce received concerning constructive trust. Remember, she was not following a bond registry protocol when she received this. She was simply in intercession for the ministry.

Malcolm's Instruction

Stephanie and I had some questions about constructive trusts, so we engaged with Heaven and Malcolm joined us. I asked, "Malcolm, could you teach us about constructive trusts?"

He replied, "I'm glad you asked me about that, Ron."

He smiled and said, "As tangible as that water is,[16] water that you feel in your hands, water that you touch every day with tangibleness, and as embers are to the fire—so is the Father's constructive love as a foundation for His people."

As he spoke, he showed Stephanie a house under construction. He continued, "Before the foundations of the world, the Lord knew the enemy would steal from his people in every *dynamic* way possible. The Father constructed, at the beginning of time, *ways and means* as an escape from the hands of the enemy."

Proceeding, Malcolm explained, "The Father knows the enemy's plans. Nothing is kept secret from Him

---

[16] Prior to this portion of the engagement, he had presented a river of water to us.

because he is not bound by time. He knew the enemy would construct consequential liens and ungodly trusts against what He has established for His sons. Every good gift is from the Father, and this is a good gift. These are the ways and means by which a strong foundation is established for people to glean from. This is part of the finished work. This is theirs for the taking. These constructive trusts will minimize and extinguish the enemy's hands. It is the undoing. It is the unweaving."

Stephanie exclaimed, "Thank you, Malcolm! Can you tell us—is this like Godly bonds, and how will we be using this?"

Malcolm answered, "The Godly bonds are imperative—particularly important. They are part of this work; however, these constructive trusts are like a nail in the coffin to the enemy."

Stephanie asked, "As people pull the tab forward to see consequential liens, is this a part of that as well?"

"Yes," he replied.

Stephanie said, "Malcolm is showing me that these constructive trusts are like Godly bonds; these are gifts that Holy Spirit, Wisdom, Understanding, and Counsel will give to us through understanding constructive trusts." We had previously been told to invite Wisdom to accompany us and to hold our hand through this process.

Stephanie described what she was seeing, "I just saw land, a chasm, and then more land; and I saw Malcolm with a steel cable. He was pulling the cable and bringing the land masses together."

Malcolm stated, "That is what this is going do—bridge the divide. It is that strong; it is strength. Its strength is palpable."

Stephanie asked, "How can we get our hands on this cable to use this?"

He responded, "Don't you already know how to use Godly bonds?"

"Yes," she answered. Then Stephanie mused, "Malcolm, to get this revelation, we have walked it. We have walked in this. We have studied this, and we have been doing this on behalf of people. It is solid ground in our hearts. This is the next step."

I agreed, "We will request these like Joyce did."

Stephanie asked, "Malcolm, why did you just say, 'The strength of this is numbers?' Do you mean strength in numbers? What does that mean?"

Malcolm answered, "There are more constructive trusts than there are consequential liens upon people's lives. Father always gives more. He pours out more. He loves more. This is His favor. Many think they do not walk in favor. Imagine this favor upon them. Imagine them seeing this favor upon them, as a king would have favor on his natural son."

Stephanie said, "He is showing me that we cannot even think or imagine the favor we have as His spiritual sons. This is part of that scripture—we 'can't even think or imagine,'[17] isn't it, Malcolm?"

At this point we were pointed to use the information that Joyce gleaned from her encounter with Heaven that introduced us to constructive trusts.

Favor is key.

Malcolm said, "The people need to understand that they are favored and that this is a gift from Holy Spirit."

I asked, "What else do we need to know about it, Malcolm?"

Stephanie replied, "I see Joyce speaking in tongues as she is walking through this process and the revelation is coming. It is like a word of knowledge is coming out of the speaking in tongues. I am watching her do that. We are not afraid to speak in tongues in front of the clients."

Malcolm stated, "Consider that a QuickGuide."[18]

Constructive Trusts QuickGuide

Father, I request access to the Court of Records to request a constructive trust.

---

[17] 1 Corinthians 2:9, Isaiah 64:4, Ephesians 3:20
[18] QuickGuides are templates I have developed for various Courts of Heaven processes.

Father, I request the following constructive trusts:

(Simply follow Holy Spirit's instruction. For example, in Joyce's initial engagement, she requested the following constructive trusts: Constructive Trust of Unity, Constructive Trust of Racial Harmony & Freedom, Constructive Trust of Brotherhood and Sisterhood in Christ, Constructive Trust of One race, one blood)

(Watch for the paperwork to be issued from the court.)

I request the constructive trusts be established for the following:

(Name the person[s] or entities to be the beneficiaries of the trusts.)

I receive the constructive trust now, in Jesus' name.

I request the assistance of the angels of the Trust Department to administer the constructive trust, like a sheet or platform to the realms involved, completely, accurately, securely, and firmly.

Thank You, Lord, for what was received.

———·———

Chapter 6
Wisdom's House

Immediately after an engagement with Malcolm, we were inside Wisdom's house. Stephanie described what was occurring, "We are being asked to sit at her table. She pulled a chair back for each of us. It's a round table; it reminds me of sitting in a garden having tea."

Stephanie released what Wisdom said to me, "You are being entrusted with The Wisdom of Ages. The Father has longed for the release of this. There is a trust (and she just laughed, for it is another play on words with that), that has been invoked upon you and with Wisdom and Understanding there will be simplicity with this. Part of the procedure in this is to invite her into the process when we specifically go to look at the Generational column of the ungodly parameters. This is an instruction for her invitation by us every time. That will create the ease. Thank you, Wisdom."

She got up and put her right hand on my shoulder as she was standing behind me and said, "I have entrusted you with The Wisdom of Ages."

Stephanie said, "She's showing me that some of the hidden things in the book of Daniel are being played out through this. This is an in time and out of time revelation and it needs to be treated as such. In doing this work, you will do this *in time* and *out of time* and *in every age* and *dimension* on *behalf of the realms of the peoples.*"

"She just said it again," Stephanie announced, "This is The Wisdom of Ages created before the beginning of time—for time, for this time, for this age, for the people, because of the Son, because of the Father's love. Thank you. Thank you, Father."

Stephanie continued, "Now I'm seeing that she has walked us over to her wall which is made of pearls. There are all sizes—some very large, others medium-sized, and others quite small. I'm seeing inside of each pearl it's as if I'm looking at every person on earth in their timeline. It's like I'm looking at their specific life and looking into their dimension."

Wisdom said, "Oh, how I have longed to be invited into their situations."

Stephanie and I both said, "We invite you into mine."

Stephanie resumed sharing what she was hearing, "This is why it is important and relevant that as we do this parameter work, Wisdom is invited."

Admitting that she was having a bit of a struggle understanding the term "parameters," Wisdom handed her a plateful of little petit fours and in each one of them was a pearl. She said, "You are going to digest it. It is going to be a digestion within you, and because you've invited me, I am going to walk you through this as you digest it because you have been entrusted with The Wisdom of Ages."

Stephanie replied, "Thank you, Wisdom, for allowing me to even have a seat at the table."

Wisdom responded, "You have it because you keep inviting me into your situations."

Again, Stephanie replied, "Thank you, Wisdom."

As we walked out the door, she patted us both on the head and laughed, "You have some things to digest."

Stephanie described the petit fours saying, "These little petit fours are about this big (fashioning her fingers into a small square about two inches by two inches). They are completely iridescent. They are outlined in solid white, and I can see the pearl inside of them, but I can also see what I would think of as the texture of caramel on the inside of it, but it's not the color of caramel. On top of them they have a beautiful scrolling, like intricate artwork."

> *In wisdom's house you'll find delightful treasures and the oil of the Holy Spirit. But the stupid squander what they've been given. (Proverbs 21:20 TPT)*

Chapter 7
Red & Black Capture Bags

Stephanie and I had engaged Heaven and Ezekiel appeared carrying a red bag. We asked, "Why is it red?"

Red Capture Bags

He answered, "It is red because of the blood of Jesus."

We asked, "What is that you are carrying?"

"It's a capturing bag," Ezekiel informed us.

"What have you captured?" We inquired.

"Infiltration," he asserted.

"Well, thank you," we said.

We sensed that he wanted to teach us about capture bags, so we welcomed his instruction, and he began.

"These capturing bags are very important to be released and commissioned to the angels. The size of them matters. Begin to see, as you release capturing bags, the various sizes. There will be different sizes for different means. The one I am carrying is a large size, it was a large infiltration, and it was necessary and needed for this specific capture. There are other capturing nets/capturing bags that will be of different colors."

"I'm seeing them presented as blue and green, there is gold, there is also orange and purple," Stephanie described.

Ezekiel continued, "Each one of those represents not only a color, but a size, depending upon the capture needed. Equip the angels with all the sizes. They are representative of a specific task, and it is what they use for specific captures.

"The one that has red, representing having the blood of Jesus infused in it, was needed and necessary to keep the capture of this infiltration in it."

"Ezekiel," Stephanie asked, "What will you do with that bag?"

"We will destroy it. There's a never-ending supply of the different sizes that represent the colors of the bags," Ezekiel informed us.

He continued, "These capturing bags are not new to angels, but they are new to you regarding the different sizes and their meanings."

He began to describe the use of the bags. "This will be an important part that the ecclesia/the people need to understand while commissioning their angels. It's a tool.

"There are many different classifications of capturing bags in Heaven. There are some that are classifications for small demons—things that are easily captured or easily contained. Then there are some that are classified specifically for domains. It will capture a whole domain. This is where the fun begins when capturing domains.

"The authority that you have through Jesus enables you to commission us in the capturing of these domains—the collapsing of these domains. Other angels will be around with other classifications of these capturing bags, capturing the entities trying to flee. This is a part of a strategy of Heaven given to the saints to walk in freedom—to walk in their freedom and victory."

I had a question for clarification, "When we commission with all the sizes of bags, do we also commission with the colors?"

He replied, "Right now you will commission with the classifications. Request all the classifications of the capture bags. Later, I will teach about the different classifications that are represented as colors. But today I have taught you about this one—this red one. This is one of the larger ones. It is not the one for domains, but it is used for infiltrations."

Capture Bag Commission

Ezekiel had captured a deep penetration that was trying to impact the ministry. He captured it (in coordination with his ranks, and commanders), and they used the red classification of bag.

The day prior to this, one of our intercessors had sensed an infiltration trying to take place. We asked if what he had captured was that infiltration, and Ezekiel replied, "Yes."

Ezekiel continued, "The enemy will continue to try to infiltrate. That is why the classification of these bags is so important and the commissioning of the angels is so important. The people's commissioning of their angels with these is so important. It will prevent the infiltration into their own lives.

"You have heard of worm holes. That is a type of infiltration. These are the things we use as a tool, as a part of the dismantling of those infiltrations."

We asked, "Would you assist us in a commissioning?"

"Yes," he replied. He was already expecting that question.

Stephanie led the way:

I call Ezekiel, his commanders, and his ranks, along with my angels to come near.

Father, I request on behalf of the angels, all the different sizes, classifications, and colors of every capturing bag needed to serve the Kingdom of Heaven and to serve your people in Jesus' name.

Ezekiel, I commission you, your commanders, and your ranks to use the classifications of every capturing bag needed; to go and capture the infiltrations; to use the different colors and classifications of the bags as needed from the smallest demon to the largest domain, in the name of Jesus; to use these capturing bags throughout our realms and over LifeSpring, Sandhills Ecclesia, CourtsNet, and the other facets of LifeSpring and also those that are at work on behalf of these ministries and for their families, in Jesus' mighty name.

Ezekiel stated, "Yes, for their families, because this is a type of covering."

Stephanie remarked, "I just saw him now—in his right hand he has laid out flat every single color, and I can see them like stacked one on top of the other. He is taking them, and he has folded them up in his hand and turning around and leaving with that bag that he captured an infiltration in.

With that, Ezekiel was finished with this brief training on capture bags.

Black Capture Bags

Stephanie and I were in a classroom this day engaging with Ezekiel when the walls changed colors and were now black.

Stephanie had asked earlier when we were introduced to our first red capture bag, "Is it used for witchcraft?"

Ezekiel replied regarding that particular color of capture bag, "No, we use the black one for witchcraft."

Ezekiel continued, "As you know, witchcraft is prominent in the land and many peoples are used. The exploration of witchcraft is ancient and its usefulness to people is so misleading. It so captivates their hearts to darkness. This black capturing bag is significant where the realms of darkness are used for sorcery, witchcraft, Luciferianism, and Satanism.

"When these bags are presented to the peoples, there will be an understanding that there has been witchcraft at work, but the capturing of these things is easy. We plunder this regularly. Infiltrations, witchcraft, sorcery, Luciferianism, and Satanism will all be easily captured in these bags. Use them. They are your tools.

"When you have been an alerted that there have been possible infiltrations, witchcraft, and sorcery, these are the tools we will use. We will capture them."

Stephanie inquired, "Ezekiel, will you plunder with these bags too?"

He replied, "We will, but there are other bags we use for plunder."

Chapter 8
Silver & Gold Capture Bags

A few days after seeing our first capture bag, Stephanie and I stepped into Heaven to learn some more about them. We were taken to an office and the first thing Stephanie noticed was the color of the walls which were golden-yellow.

Golden Glory Bags

Stephanie asked, "Lydia (a woman in white who advises our ministry), are you going to teach us about the significance of these colors? What is the significance of this golden yellow?"

Lydia answered, "This is how glory presents itself to the human eye.

"Did you know there are Glory bags too?" she asked.

"No," we answered. We did not know that.

Lydia continued, "There are capturing bags and there are bags of Glory. These also can be administered by the angels into people's realm."

Lydia said, "Dr. Ron, you know about the Glory and how it is administered."

Stephanie commented, "I see us taking these bags and stepping into them and pulling them up around us. It's all encompassing. It surrounds us.

"We can release Glory like we would release Godly bonds to people. It's something that we can release on behalf of people. It will be something that you commission their angels to bring to them. It is a part of awakening their angels, stirring them up, working on behalf of those that come for prayer and for ministry."

Silver Capture Bags

A few days prior in an engagement with Heaven, we had been in a ballroom. On this engagement, we found ourselves back in the same room. This time, however, only a few balls were bouncing around in the room. Stephanie saw a few balls of assorted colors, lying on the floor (the same colors as some of the capture bags we had learned about previously). A silvery looking ball captured her attention and had a knowing that the silvery ball would be the topic of discussion today.

Malcolm, who was with us in the ballroom went over to the whiteboard. As we had been learning about different colors of capture bags and their uses, he correlated the color of the silver ball to silver capturing bags. He began, "This bag, too, is aerodynamic. **It swiftly contains. It does not primarily capture like the other bags you have learned about. Instead, this one, like the Glory bag, contains something to be released to others.**

> *This silver bag contains the essence of the Father—the essence of Holy Spirit, and what it contains will bring the evidence of that in people's lives—*
> *the essence of the Father,*
> *the strength of the Father,*
> *the goodness of the Father, the plans of the Father, the need of the Father, the value of worship of the Father, and the friendship of the Father.*

"These are necessary things that people have been missing in their lives. The use of these bags is also for the generations. It is used in generational work."

Stephanie asked, "Can you show me more? Can you make this clearer—how this essence of the Father and Holy Spirit in the use of the silver capture bags are used for the Body of Christ? Tell me about the essence of the Father."

Malcolm replied, "Many like the simplicities and the simplistic ways that they can utilize tools of the Kingdom.

That is what these are. That is what these bags are. People can mentally and visually speak and see these things as a helpful tool on their behalf—the simplicity of it. When people are praying it is a boldness, a feeling of accomplishment, a sense of the co-laboring, and that they are useful in the co-laboring with the angels. They are gaining strength from it, and they are seeing results."

Malcolm began showing Stephanie a picture of a person in prayer asking of the Father on behalf of the angels for the silver bags. "These are not capturing bags in the sense most of the other bags are, they are bags that contain the essence of the Father—all those things mentioned above—to be given to that person. It acts like a bonding agent, like a bond. A play on words, right?" Malcolm suggested.

Stephanie asked, "Can this be a bond that is released?"

Malcolm replied, "It is. It can be. When it is apropos meaning when it is relevant and opportune or an opportune time to do so. It is the right thing for the right time.

"As a simple instruction, when they are praying on behalf of someone, have them say, 'As an act of faith take that silver bag to yourself.' Many have missed the relational side of prayer. Many can visually experience the relationship.

> *They can physically experience the relationship of the Father as this tool is used by the body.*

"This unsophisticated action shows the simplicity of Heaven, yet it is profound love and favor for the body and for the peoples. Think of it as an act of love and in turn, your release of that on behalf of someone else is also an act of love—love for your neighbor, love for your friend, love for family, love for the Body of Christ.

"Use this diligently. Use it often. The essence of the Father and His love will settle upon the peoples. There will be a fragrance about it—an enhancement because of it, a beauty around it, and a just cause will bear witness from it. Use this in your courtroom work. It is tangible. Its immediate effects will be known as the effective fervent prayers of a righteous man will avail much.[19]

I said, "Well, let us just receive the silver bag."

Stephanie began, "The silver bags, I receive it into my realms. It is tangible."

She asked Malcolm, "Is this is something we can release to a believer who is struggling?"

"Yes," he replied. "It is very much like how a bond works. This can be released for those who do not understand this prayer paradigm, who need the essence

---

[19] James 5:16

of the Father, His love, His friendship, and it will be astounding to them."[20]

Stephanie inquired, "Malcolm, if I am praying on behalf of someone, and they do not know that I am praying for them, this is released?"

He declared, "Think of it as a drawing near that they will experience."

She remarked, "That is good, Malcolm. It is a beautiful picture, Malcolm. This is like the Glory bag. I just saw myself receiving the contents of the silver bag and holding the Glory bag that I want to step into."

"They are containers to be released?" she asked.

"Yes, these two bags are containers of the Glory of the Father and the essence and love of the Father that need to be released to people," he replied.

She asked, "Are they also containers to gather?"

He replied, "That is right. You will utilize them to gather people into the Glory and the essence and love of the Father."

More on the Glory Bags

Stephanie said, "He is showing me that sometimes people get caught up in words when they are hearing people talk about the Glory. They have not ascertained

---

[20] We can also request the any of the bags for ourselves.

how to utilize it for themselves. This is a simplistic, loving way that people can use their imaginations to utilize it for themselves, and as they pray for others. Thank you for that, Malcolm."

At that moment we had a brief interruption with a situation with a client. We asked that she receive this silver bag to show her the essence of who the Father is.

As soon as Stephanie made the request, she saw her LHS (Lingering Human Spirit) Hotel[21] full of occupants, and they were requesting on behalf of themselves that the angels would bring them the silver bags while they are at the hotel reading their Destiny in Heaven book and listening to Adina's music.[22]

Malcolm handed Stephanie a bunch of silver bags and said, "You can absolutely take them to the hotel."

Stephanie asked a question of Malcolm, "Does the gold Glory bag simply contains the Glory of God to be released to people?"

He said, "Yes. Would you like one?"

"Oh yes," I replied.

Changing subjects slightly, Stephanie asked, "Do you have more to tell us about the silver bags, Malcolm,"

---

[21] Stephanie has created in her realm a gathering place for LHS's that are wanting to transition to Heaven. She refers to it as her hotel.
[22] This is explained in the second edition of the book, *Lingering Human Spirits*, set to be released in the Spring of 2022.

Malcolm replied, "When those who struggle when they hear these messages, that struggle believing falsely, that they themselves cannot ascertain the Glory or ascertain the love and the essence of the Father, these are great tools for them, for their behalf, and on their behalf. They *can* imagine. They *can see* whether they are a seer or not and can understand what a bag looks like, feels like, and *can* imagine themselves stepping into the Glory with the use of the tool that is the Glory bag. They *can* ascertain the essence and the experience of it with the tool that is the silver bag.

"Simplicity is needed at times, and at times these tools are needed. Make skillful use of them for they are for your benefit because of the Father's love. Because you have said yes to co-laboring with angels, this is a direct result and a benefit of that. It is a reminder that angels are not just useful in battle, but they are useful in the presentation of the Father's love and of His Glory and of His Kingdom."

Stephanie observed, "Now I am in the Court of Angels, and I see all these angels with both gold and silver bags in hand."

"Can we commission you to take these silver bags to those who have drawn near the ministry?" she inquired.

Immediately, the answer was, "Yes!" and instantly, the angels took flight.

Ezekiel then appeared and was covered in gold dust. We asked what he had been doing and were told he had been delivering Glory bags to people on behalf of the ministry.

He began saying, "It has been a great honor to deliver these bags and all their benefits to those that have drawn close to the ministry and especially on behalf of those who work for the ministry. It is the Father's love. Great benefit comes from loving the Father and choosing His Kingdom. These are Kingdom benefits. Look at them like that. Teach the people Kingdom benefits. Align yourself with the Kingdom of Heaven. As simple as this may seem, it will work profoundly in your lives. The Father smiles down upon this ministry."

The Essence and the Glory

This day, when we engaged Heaven, we were taken upstairs to a different room, one wall of which was a view of outer space. We were seated at a table with a white flame hovering above the table. Joseph (a man in white linen) spoke, "This is a picture of what the Essence and the Glory look like together—a pure white light."

The light then leapt off the table and into outer space.

Joseph continued, "His Glory and His essence upon the earth, upon men's hearts, upon their realms, shall be evident just as you see the flame, just as in the day when

Holy Spirit came, and flames were seen above the people.[23] The essence will rest upon the people."

Then he said, "Walk with me. As you see the rushing of the waters, you will see the Essence of the Glory light upon people."

He stopped at a brook, and referring to an engagement David, Stephanie, and I had the prior day, he said, "The baptismal pool you saw is an invitation not just to Sandhills Ecclesia, but to all who draw close to the ministry, to step into the water which contains the Essence of His Glory—there will be an evidence upon their lives. You will *see* the evidence. This is the goodness of Heaven. The early believers experienced the evidence of speaking a language heretofore unknown to them. Heaven is going to do this marvelous thing."

We were then transported back to a different room. Jason, a man in white linen, was present to assist us. He brought an ancient book. On the cover was a large medallion and Jason took a sword and inserted it into the keyhole that was in the medallion and turned the sword like a key. As he did, Stephanie could hear the sound of the unlocking of the lock mechanism. The book was entitled, *The Book of Numbers*. Stephanie asked if this was "a" book of numbers, or "the" Book of Numbers. She was assured it was the latter and suggested we turn to Numbers 4. Jason began helping unpack information in that passage and later in chapter 27, which spoke of

---

[23] Acts 2:3

inheritance. A principle of inheritance was unveiled that is simply:

> *An inheritance may be distributed,*
> *but to have benefit,*
> *it must be possessed.*

The passage in Numbers 27 spoke of those who were to carry the presence.

Jason said, "Each of you, each of your realms, carries the tabernacle within you. You are a type and shadow of the tabernacle, the holy that lives within you—the essence—the glory you carry within you. There are those in need that need this Essence and this Glory. It will shine and be evident upon each of you. They will see it. They will know it. They will want it and desire it."

Stephanie spoke, "I have a question, Jason. So those of us that are spirit-filled and have been spirit-filled, we have been carrying around the Glory and this Essence. Are you saying that what we are walking into now, this new revelation, this new impartation contains new evidence of what is coming? Or what people will see?"

He replied, "The flame that they see upon you will be so evident that many will be drawn to it, and it will alight upon others."

Stephanie explained, "He just showed me a picture of how when there is a fire, embers come off of it and go to something nearby, lighting something on fire. This is the kind of evidence we will see. Now, I'm seeing an entire forest fire, but in a good way.

"Jason, this teaching, this revelation—is this about those that are or will be filled with the Holy Spirit?"

I interjected, "Since Jason is referring to the fire so much, are we referring to the baptism of Holy Spirit *and* fire? Is that what he's alluding to?"

He confirmed, "Great question, Ron. That's exactly what this is. Because the Essence and the Glory is what creates the fire. The fire is the Essence *and* the Glory combined."

Stephanie reported, "He's showing that we have learned about the Glory, and we learned yesterday about the Essence along with the silver bags that contain the Essence. We have also been given the gold bags that contain the Glory, and he's saying, 'Imagine the two of them together,' so when we release these for people and on behalf of people, contained within them and combined together is the fire."

> *Moses brought their case before the Lord. ⁶ And the Lord spoke to Moses saying ⁷ the daughters of Zelophedad speak what is right; you shall surely give them a possession of inheritance among their father's brothers, and cause the inheritance of their father to pass to them. (Numbers 27:5)*

Jason said, "Just like in Numbers 27 where the Lord laid out what inheritances were for the people on our earth, this is an inheritance. This is the truest form of inheritance from the Father. His Glory and His Essence combined, bringing the fire upon the people, lighting the fire within them, dwelling upon them, and being so evident, people are drawn to the light—the flame.

"There was a parallel that they showed us just now of in the beginning when the Lord set up the inheritance in the natural using the Courts of Heaven, there's an inheritance for us in the spiritual. Here, this inheritance must not only be distributed, but it also must be possessed. The sword of the Lord, it is your strength; and Wisdom is who is at your right hand. The Glory and the Essence that will be upon you brings the fire of the Lord."

Ezekiel then appeared with two bags over his shoulders—a gold bag over one shoulder and a silver bag over the other shoulder with a small flame in his hand.

Stephanie asked, "Ezekiel, are you saying this is the new walk, the new beginning on behalf of this ministry for the peoples and for the Kingdom, with new insight and new understanding all gained from the seat of rest? All of it because He loves us?"

He replied, "This flame will be evident upon you just as it is evident in my hand. As the Father releases His glory and His essence upon the people, and what you described as an ember, it will be a movement."

Stephanie remarked, "When he said the word 'movement.' I saw the movement of rushing water and then I saw the movement as a frequency."

Ezekiel continued, "This is what the earth groans for. An innumerable number of angels carry this. They carry this torch. They carry this flame which is being released for such a time as this. It will grow just as a natural fire grows and will spread. This will spread. This will bring people from the North, South, East, and West."

Stephanie explained, "I just saw a picture of the whole earth and people coming from every continent and place. Do we need to commission you to this work on behalf of the people of LifeSpring?"

"Yes," he declared.

Stephanie began:

I commission you in the name of Jesus, Ezekiel, with your commanders, and ranks on behalf of the people, those who have drawn near to the ministry, those who work for the ministry, and their families, to bring the flame that is the Essence and the Glory of the Father upon the people. That it may spread like embers and light upon the people so that all may see that it as evidence, as the Father has said that it would be in evidence.

We commission you to the full use of the silver and the gold bags that carry the Essence and carry the Glory, and to bring them to everyone's realms in the name of Jesus.

Father, I would like for Understanding to go with this commissioning that is being released—this fire.

"I'm seeing Understanding playing a big part of this," she remarked. "It's the first time I've seen him as an entity that leaves and goes like that."

Continuing the commission, she spoke,

Father, we request that Understanding be released for all of those that hear, that draw near, that seek the Kingdom of God, and we release you, Ezekiel, your commanders, and ranks to do this good work on behalf of the Father, in Jesus' name.

With that, Ezekiel turned and left.

Welcoming Understanding

Lydia, who had been quietly standing to the side then stepped up and said, "Speaking of Understanding,[24] much understanding will come from this. Be patient. Just be patient. This is a new level. A new place. Understanding will come. Understanding is going to be playing a very large role at this level."

Stephanie said, "Understanding, I welcome you in everything and just like I hold Wisdom's hand. I want to hold your hand."

---

[24] Understanding is an entity as well as a capability.

Lydia continued, "There are new frequencies being released upon the earth through these messages; frequencies that are so supernatural, that Understanding being released upon them is what is going to bring this understanding of this frequency to their ears. Just like the flame and the embers, you will see it grow among the people quickly."

Stephanie responded, "We welcome all of this. Lydia, we welcome what Heaven has to bring through this ministry on behalf of the Kingdom of Heaven. I ask for clarity for me and for Ron, for all of this understanding as we piece this puzzle together."

Malcolm (who had been silently watching) came close. I had earlier asked if we would understand more of the capture bags that we had yet to be introduced to and he had no reply. I asked him, "Is there anything else we need for the book?"

He replied, "Essence? It's an entire world." With that he left the room.

I took a moment to look at the definition of "essence."[25] It is quite interesting. "The intrinsic nature or indispensable quality of something that determines its character, especially something abstract."

The philosophy definition was "The inherent unchanging nature of a thing or class of things, especially as contrasted with its existence," and also "a property or

---

[25] Google's English Dictionary definition of essence

group of properties of something without which it would not exist or be what it is." An additional definition said, "An extract or concentrate obtained from a particular plant or other matter and used for flavoring or scent. It creates a frequency."

"The most significant element, quality, or aspect of a thing or person in concentrated form or substance as of a perfume."

"Something that exists, an entity."

Wikipedia[26] had an interesting definition. "Essence. It's a polysomic term using philosophy and theology as a designation for the property or set of properties that make an entity or substance what it fundamentally is and which it has by necessity and without which it loses its identity."

---

[26] Wikipedia definition of essence

Chapter 9
Purple Capture Bags

Stephanie and I had been engaging Heaven and learning about capture bags. In this meeting, the walls would change color based on the topic of discussion.

Deep Purple Capture Bags

Stephanie noted a change and described it, "Now the room has switched to purple—like deep purple. The walls are very dark in this purple color. It is very beautiful, and it has flashes of light through it, all over the walls like there were mirrors on the walls reflecting light."

They explained, "This deep royal purple is the next step down from the red capture bags."

Stephanie asked, "Can you tell me what its purpose is for?"

Ezekiel explained, "It's another size. **It goes into dimensions. It's what is needed and useful when going into other times and dimensions.** It prevents what is captured from escaping when they are taking them out of other times and dimensions. It's lined with the authority that is interwoven into the fabric of the bag, but it's a grid. It is a very useful tool. As you know, we will be doing many things in time and out of time, and this is the purpose of this specific capturing bag."

Stephanie quizzed him, "Ezekiel, is this when we commission our angels? Are we to use the full commissioning of a capturing bag of every size, color, and dimension?"

He said, "Yes, but what we are teaching now is their usefulness and why they are different colors and sizes."

She asked, "Ezekiel, will people be confused by it? The very first one you showed us was the red for the blood of Jesus. Will that be confusing to them that there are different colors?"

He clarified, "The blood is upon all of these, the name above all names, and the authority is upon all of these. These colors are for your uses, for your knowledge and understanding. You will see them play out as you work in this paradigm of prayer using these capturing bags. You will know specifically when I come with a specific color bag what has been captured, whether it's an infiltration, whether it's black for witchcraft, or whether it's this deep, royal purple which is where something was caught in a different time, age, and dimension for your knowledge. This is the wisdom of Heaven and because of the Father's love for you, He wants you to know all these things."

As he turned around to leave, Stephanie noticed a red capture bag on his shoulder. Apparently, he had captured a couple of infiltrations, one of which was stuffed in a purple bag which was stuffed inside the larger red bag.

Stephanie said, "You have captured one in time and out of time—is that correct?"

He replied, "Yes."

We asked, "Is there anything we need to know regarding that?"

He said, "No, it is the splendid work of the intercessors. Tell them."

"We will," we replied, "we will."

——— · ———

Chapter 10
Green, Blue & Grey Capture Bags

Continuing the engagement, the room suddenly changed colors to green. Ezekiel explained, "These are the plunder bag colors. The green represents the wealth, and the sevenfold return of things stolen. We can use them in tandem as we plunder the kingdoms of darkness."

Green Capture Bags

Stephanie remarked, "Ezekiel this is useful information."

He expounded, "We give it because the Father loves the authority that you stand in and the co-laboring with us as angels. He gives this information because He loves this—the awakening of His children, the hunger for knowledge, the hunger for Heaven, the hunger for Him. It is His great pleasure. It is His joy."

Again, we thanked him, and Ezekiel took a step back.

Malcolm came forward and said, **"The lessons in leaning in our paradigms of prayer is when we can call upon the angels to use these capturing bags during those times of attack as well, especially the release of the Glory bags for the people.** They work in tandem when we call upon the angels to silence the principalities.

"The end product of this is the usefulness with the angels, the co-laboring, the capturing bags, the Glory bags.

It is the quick silencing of the enemy, and the opening of the Kingdom Dynamics of Heaven.

"Our realms—who you are, how God created you—include mountains, even things you don't understand—it is a landscape, which is why the principalities consider it a region. This is why it takes place with a consequential lien. Your footsteps on the earth create your region upon the earth."

Stephanie asked, "Is there anything else about capturing bags or lessons on leaning?"

Describing what she was seeing, she said, "A brilliantly shining bright orb appeared."

Wisdom explained, "This for the light of what is coming." Four books were on the table, the Book of LifeSpring, the Book of Sandhills Ecclesia, the Book of

CourtsNet, and the BAS Global[27] Book were all on the table.

Stephanie described the scene, "This orb, as it comes closer to the table, is growing in size. It's one of the brightest things I've ever seen. It's hovering above all four books. The only thing I can describe is like those old shows about Frankenstein, where they had that big globe that had lightning coming out of it. That is what this looked like to me. The power is going into the books—this electricity, this frequency, this lightning is going into all the books, but it is also hovering above it."

She asked, "What is it?"

Malcolm replied, "It is knowledge. It is integrity. It is wisdom. It is lightning-force swift action upon the hearts of man that come into this teaching. It is Kingdom Dynamics. It is because we pray Your Kingdom come, Your will be done. It is ultimately His will. That's what this orb is—His will. You can think of it in those terms.

"Yes. There are many aspects to what you are seeing come out of this as His will. It is because the Kingdom is at hand."

Stephanie described, "I'm just watching this just pour into all the books."

---

[27] BAS (Business Advocate Services), now known as Heaven Down Business, is an extension of LifeSpring.

Malcolm kept saying, "This is the structure from now on."

She asked, "Are you saying, because of obedience, prayer, and all the things you've shown us before, that His will is evident in all four of these?"

He replied, "Yes, but His will is evident. It is a pouring out of all those things mentioned in these books that will affect the people as it reflects the ministry, which reflects His will because of praying for His Kingdom to come.

Stephanie described what was happening, "Everyone one who had joined us began leaving the room, but the books were still open. It is like it will be here from this point forward and they just showed me another book that's coming. We had seen the books for LifeSpring, CourtsNet, Heaven Down Business, and Sandhills Ecclesia. This one was more darkened and not opened yet. Apparently, that is to come.

The Commissioning

I call Ezekiel, his commanders, and his ranks, along with my angels to come near. Father, I request on behalf of the angels, all the different sizes, classifications, and colors of every capturing bag needed to serve the Kingdom of Heaven and to serve your people, in Jesus' name.

Ezekiel, I commission you, your commanders, and your ranks to use the classifications of every capturing bag needed to go and capture the infiltrations, to use the different colors and classifications of the bags as needed from the smallest demon to the largest domain in the name of Jesus.

I also request of the Father, Glory bags for distribution to the saints hearing this message.

I commission you to the full use of these Glory bags for the Glory of the Father in the lives of His sons and daughters in Jesus' name.

Blue Capture Bags

We were desiring instruction about blue capture bags, which typically appeared much smaller than some other capture bags we had seen.

Describing what she was hearing, Stephanie said, "Hey Malcolm, I'm hearing two words. I'm hearing 'paradigm,' and I'm hearing 'perplexed.' Can you teach us what that is?"

He responded by taking this bag he had drawn on the whiteboard, and he drew arrows to the right of it. He said, **"This bag captures the enemy's weapons."**

Stephanie said, "He showed me the arrows as twofold arrows—as weapons with the arrows pointing to the word 'paradigm.'"

Malcolm said, "It is perplexing to us about how the enemy has weapons." He said, "Satan is a legalist, but he is also a copycat. His falsehood presents weaponry as we would in the natural think of weaponry, but his weapons *are only tactics*. This has perplexed us in that, in the natural, we think of him attacking us with weapons— his weapons are also words and lies— tactical strategies of deception. These blue bags will capture the paradigms that perplex us."

We noted, "That's a lot of P words Malcolm."

He continued, "When it comes to the enemy's warfare and talking about arrows, your armor will deflect the arrows from the enemy."

Stephanie said, "I always assumed they were actual weapons. I saw them as actual arrows."

Malcolm continued, "Their words or strategies inflict more damage than a natural arrow ever could upon a person's realms. Capture the accusations. In this paradigm, I'm telling you that you don't have to get caught up in saying, 'Angels, go and capture the words and the phrases and the strategies.' We can say, 'Capture the accusations.' We can do that before the enemy has a legal right to bring it to the Courts of Heaven against us. This is the sovereignty of God on behalf of His sons."

Narrating what was now depicted to her, Stephanie reported, "I'm seeing Jacob's ladder and how the accuser goes to ascend and descend a ladder to bring accusations against us. Sometimes, the enemy comes to us personally, speaking to us— where to accuse ourselves, where we accuse others in our hearts and our mind. It is not a sin *until we embrace it,* and *we act upon it.*"

Stunned by what she was hearing, Stephanie asked, "Are you telling me that this can be done to prevent those words and accusations from the enemy reaching our spirit and our heart and our soul?"

In response he showed Stephanie Jacob's ladder again, with the enemy going up and down, and said, "This is simple."

I remarked, "Our repentance is for the entertaining of these accusations against others and against ourselves, et cetera."

Stephanie continued, "He just showed me what happens before the enemy can go upon the ladder (all this was simply a visual to help us understand). Before the enemy is able to take it to the Courts of Heaven to accuse us, where we must come into agreement with the accuser, the step before that is when we come into agreement— we hear it, and we take it on. That is when he can have a legal right.

Malcolm explained, "These capture bags are a part of the paradigms of prayer to forfeit the enemy's legal right to form accusations against us. This is a gift."

Stephanie, remembering she had heard the word 'sovereignty' wondered how it fit in with what we were learning.

Malcolm replied, "What this bag is for is a prevention of the next step of the enemy against us, which is where we would come into agreement or take on the accusation. It circumvents that for us because we are His kids. He is the one who has simplified this aspect, so we are not dealing with accusations over and over repeatedly. Heaven is simply taking that out of the equation for us."

He leaned over and said, "Look how the Father loves. That is what this is. He is giving us this tool. It's like a preventative medicine. It is for dismantling something before it begins. It's a preventative."

Stephanie proclaimed, "Father, thank You. I'm in awe of You. I am in awe of Your Love and Your Kingdom Tactics."

She added, "He is showing me how people have just been sick and tired of the same accusations over and over repeatedly. This tool is something we can use in our paradigms of prayer as we commission angels to use this on our behalf, where we are not accepting or falling for the enemy's tactics, but instead are being given Kingdom Tactics that are offensive instead of defensive. They are preventative measures, for us. Thank you."

Grey Capture Bags

Jeremy, one of our team members, was in prayer recently in response to a request for how to deal with a situation he was facing in his home. Jeremy and his wife parent several small children and he noticed some movies or television shows were releasing a lot of profanity into the air which was polluting the atmosphere. He heard Heaven say, "Request grey capture bags."

Asking what they did, he heard, "The grey capture bags work much like a shop vac or leaf blower that has both sucking and blowing capabilities; they have dual use. When requesting the grey capture bags, essentially your angels will be able to kill two birds with one stone."

Heaven said, "**The first component is the isolation and removal of any ungodly frequencies.**" He could see an angel holding a bag that was fully inflated and it was sucking in all the ungodly frequencies in the space in front and around of where the bag was positioned.

Heaven continued, "**The second feature is the release of Godly frequencies and the frequency of Heaven.**"

Again, he could see the angel with the bag, only this time a golden sparkling mist was being released.

He said, "It basically has dual-action cleaning power." My angel chuckled and then showed me how the ungodly frequencies can suck the life and joy out of an atmosphere and leave the people in that atmosphere feeling heavy or agitated.

He saw the scene depicting this as a vivid image that had all the color sucked out of it. The individuals in the image looked very melancholy but when the Godly frequencies were released it was like a revival breaking out, suddenly the color reappeared, more vibrant than before and everyone seemed alive with the joy of the Lord. There was also a serenity and a peace that came over the scene with the release of these Godly frequencies.

He sensed the need to request and commission his angels to use this new item for his house and family.

He prayed,

Father, in Jesus' name I request the grey capture bags for our angels and ranks and I commission our angels to use these bags to remove the ungodly frequencies and release the heavenly frequencies into our home and realms, in Jesus' name.

He asked, "Can these be used in tandem with other frequency weapons like shields and headphones. He heard, "Yes."

He asked, "Are they specifically for the frequencies of words and sound waves and again he heard, "Yes."

Adding the grey capture bags to the tool kit of Heaven known as capture bags should help the Body of Christ gain new levels of freedom. Enjoy them! Use them!

Hand in Hand with Wisdom

Stephanie and I had engaged Heaven when Wisdom appeared with a large iridescent pearl in her hand. She was turning it in her hand and reminded me that she had given me the Wisdom of Ages a few days before.

She instructed us to tell the people to invoke her; invoke Wisdom in *everything* that they do and in all the teachings that are being taught.

She said if they come to her door, request Wisdom and the angels to use the capture bags along with the extraordinary things that LifeSpring brings to people, that she will give them the Wisdom of Ages. "It is the Father's desire that you carry Wisdom— the Pearls of Wisdom around your neck."

She set that large Pearl of Wisdom on the table in front of me and said, "It is yours for the keeping. It's the continuing of the Wisdom of Ages. As I teach you, I want you to teach the people that Wisdom must be invoked— she must be invited. It is necessary."

Walking Together

Ezekiel then appeared, demonstrating how he and Wisdom walk together through things. He was demonstrating that as we teach the people about Wisdom and the need to understand all of these things— including arming your angels, co-laboring with your angels—that walking with the entity Wisdom is an important piece of the puzzle.

He showed us that he and Wisdom were holding hands and that's how he wants the people to see themselves, as holding hands with Wisdom and Wisdom holding hands with Ezekiel. This is also a representation of their own personal angels who should be commissioned to walk hand in hand with Wisdom. It's a three-cord strand.

He smiled and began to walk away hand-in-hand with Wisdom. In his other hand he slung an orange bag over his shoulder.

―――― · ――――

Chapter 11
Orange, Brown & Tan Capture Bags

Stephanie remarked, "I'm assuming we are going to learn about orange capturing bags, because as he's walking away, in his right hand he is holding and shaking an orange capturing bag." She asked, "What's that orange about?"

Orange Capture Bags

He said, "It's for domains. **Orange is the capturing of a domain.**"

She asked, "What domain was captured?"

He replied, "Domains are evil empires, evil domains. I used it in conjunction with the purple bag."

Stephanie observed, "I see purple inside of the orange bag, so this domain was in another time and dimension."

She explained, "You captured a domain— one that was encroaching upon the ministry as a whole (she had just seen all of the books together). You captured a domain that was being built by the enemy to create an illusion to other people— a false domain."

Ezekiel showed her the domain as in a computer website domain and said, "Someone was trying to create a false domain to be a replica, a duplicate of LifeSpring Ministries."

Stephanie asked, "Is this like a website domain name found on the internet?"

Ezekiel continued, "I captured it. Remember, I take these and destroy them and the bags. I will be taking it to destroy it. The domain is two-fold. The domain where someone was going to duplicate or create a false replica of LifeSpring Ministries, where when people go to a search of LifeSpring, but they were going to be taken to a different place. It was the false as well as a domain in the spiritual—a room where it was created in a different dimension in time."

"Thank you for that capture," we gratefully acknowledged.

He continued, "This came from the Strategy Room. I knew from the Strategy Room where to go to capture this domain in time and out of time, as well as taking down that platform."

We again thanked Ezekiel as he walked away having taught us even more about capture bags and the various colors.

Brown Capture Bags

Early in the day I mentioned to Stephanie that I wanted to learn more about capture bags and more about what certain colors meant. We stepped into the realms of Heaven, asking for a meeting with Malcolm. He was waiting for us in the classroom with an eraser and two pieces of chalk in his hand.

When he asked what we wanted to learn about today, we responded with an answer that we felt he already knew. We stated, "We would like to know about the different color bags."

He began by saying the word "aerodynamic."

We asked, "What can you tell us about the capturing bags that is more than we know now?"

He said, "You heard the word aerodynamics for a reason. It is their usefulness. As you see in the natural something aerodynamic, how it goes faster, it has the same usefulness that these have. Think of it in those terms."

Malcolm then began drawing on the whiteboard. He drew a big bag. The larger he drew it, the larger the whiteboard became. He became small in comparison.

Stephanie could see the rope with which angels tie these capture bags.

We asked, "What color is this bag? Or are you showing me something different?"

He said, "Size matters, so this is a very large bag. I will talk to you about size and color simultaneously."

With that, Malcolm began coloring the bag brown.

He continued, **"This captures land that was taken captive by the enemy. It is essentially 'illegal land.'"**

Stephanie could see a large land mass and even saw a castle on a high place on the land. "You're showing me a generational thing, aren't you?"

"Yes," he replied. "This is captive land taken by the enemy that belongs to the children of God—the sons of men. It is like a dominion but is not a dominion."

She asked, "Is this a dominion of evil? Is this land that people in the natural have lost or that has been stolen?"

He responded, "This is taking captive a dominion that has been encamped and has encroached upon the land. It is like a territory, but unlike the domains, which can be captured in the orange bag, it is different from that because this one deals with physical earth."

To clarify, Stephanie asked, "Is this different because it deals with physical earth or is it limited?"

"It's both," he replied.

Describing what she was seeing, Stephanie said, "I'm seeing a land mass, and then I'm also seeing it as a spiritual land mass."

"Malcolm, am I correct in seeing that this is a lien that a principality has put upon a region of land or someone's land that was stolen? Is this an encroaching of an evil dominion upon a territory?" she queried.

"Upon land," he confirmed.

Stephanie continued, "Now I'm seeing where natural land has been cursed because there has been bloodshed upon it and where land has been stolen.

"Malcolm, explain to us about this dominion, because I'm seeing it like an evil principality, with its commanders and ranks overlaid over someone's territory or land mass in the natural. Is that right?"

Malcolm acknowledged, "Yes. Like what you would hear about in the Bible of princes being over regions—like the Prince of Persia being over a region that was an entire land mass. It contained an entire body of people. These are for individuals' sakes. These are for families' sakes.

"This is land that's been stolen from people, even in the natural. Think of it as the land that the Native Americans had stolen from them. That is a dominion that has been placed over them and their heritage, an evil dominion that can be easily captured—easily dismantled."

Stephanie responded saying, "Let me ask you a question. Can repentance work that has been done concerning land that has been taken like that, can that be applied for the capture bags by simply commissioning the angels to retrieve the land and remove the captured principality?"

Malcolm explained, "The ability to remove the principality is a part of the parameter and will be a useful tool when dealing with parameters that are seen on someone's life as a trust. The Godly Trust in this as I am showing you, is all that Heaven has for us including inheritances that were stolen from us—that includes land."

Stephanie desired an illustration of what Malcolm was telling us. She began to see Kevin (one of our Senior Advocates) doing courtroom work and looking at someone's Trust Registry, realizing that there's a parameter—a consequential lien that has been placed upon land that has been stolen geographically and people groups who live on that land. She exclaimed, "He is showing it to me as masses of people and I keep seeing first peoples specifically."

I said, "Can I ask another question? Malcolm, you are aware of Mary Doe's[28] situation where she's the rightful owner of land that her siblings are trying to steal because they want to sell it at a higher price although there are

---

[28] Name has been changed to protect identity

gentlemen's agreements between them that Mary is the rightful owner."

Stephanie responded, "The minute you said her name I heard, 'This is a dominion. This is an evil dominion as a lien and a situation perfect for the use of the capture bags. I am also seeing a purple bag because it is in time and out of time. I am seeing the weaving of those two bags together as a capture bag to remove the principality that has been plaguing that family."

"Good example, Ron," Malcolm commented.

Stephanie regrouped, "Malcolm, you showed me the land mass as an actual natural land mass. I saw a coastline and a castle on a hill overlooking the ocean. I saw the whole land mass captured. Then I saw the domain overlaying the captured land mass. You are saying that the purpose of this capture bag, in use with consequential liens, is to capture the dominion and free the land mass. Is it that easy to capture the dominion?"

"Well, yes! This IS Heaven!" he exuded.

Stephanie reflected, "That is why Kevin has figured out that we're not dealing with low level demons. We are just dealing with principalities and getting it over with."

"Yes. It's that easy, yes," he confirmed.

Malcolm then showed Stephanie something else. "He keeps taking me back to the finished work of Jesus," she pondered.

"Those are the things that are still being laid out in front of us that we are under. We are just now beginning to understand the magnitude of the finished work of Jesus with the simplicity of what we have as sons of God because of His finished work and His blood that was shed. This is the work of Heaven and the Kingdom Dynamics."

Malcolm said, "This is part of the Kingdom Dynamics."

I had another question for Malcolm, "Malcolm, how does this work in relation to cities?"

He responded, "Good question, Ron. There are evil dominions who have taken over land masses and cities. Remember the Prince of Persia."

I replied, "As we're doing this work, with the capture bags that are given to the angels, is that like what was used between Gabriel and the angel that visited Daniel?"

He said, "Now you're getting the reference to the book of Daniel that I made previously. Yes, that is what was used then and that is what will be used now—a brown capture bag."

Stephanie said, "I just saw individual capture bags that were brown, related to every state, when I saw the map of the United States. I then saw dominions over each state, which is a geographical land mass. I'm also seeing smaller dominions inside those that are related to cities within the states. Now I'm seeing bloodshed."

She asked, "Is that how the dominion can take authority?"

Malcolm explained, "That is the legal right which a dominion (a prince) has for his kingdom. One of the first things to look at, when dealing with evil dominions, is bloodshed and profane worship. Yes, all the things you've been taught previously will also tie into understanding this paradigm now."

Stephanie saw this as an addendum to the teaching in my book, *Engaging the Courts for Your City*, because of the usefulness of this commissioning of angels and as the people learn to engage the watchman.

Dominions Over Oceans

He then began to show the brown bags over the seas.

He said, "Yes, over the seas and the release of LHS's."[29]

He began showing Stephanie examples of dominion over parts of the ocean. He showed her bloodshed on ships, some of whom were slaves who died on board the ships. He showed me ships that went down into the seas, that it was related to ungodly water kingdoms, and that the evil dominion had captured LHS's in that place. The work would be two-fold: Dealing with the principality through repentance for the bloodshed, et cetera, and

---

[29] Lingering Human Spirits—see the book by that name.

helping the LHS's get free and transition to Heaven. We had a recent example of that when we did some repentance work for bloodshed in Mississippi and on the Mississippi River. David Porter (one of our team members) had witnessed a piece of the Mississippi river open and hundreds of LHS's set free.

Malcolm inquired, "Are you seeing the correlation of dominions to water kingdoms?"

We asked if he had more to discuss about the brown capture bags. He showed Stephanie a picture of a little child trying to tie their shoelaces. It might take a few moments at first but eventually the child becomes very skilled at it. He said, "The work and the simplicity of tying a shoelace is the simplicity of this work."

Capturing Dominions

Wisdom turned around and walked over to the wall. Stephanie could then see the brown capture bags. They were brought into the conference room and on the bag was written 'Vital Work' in white stitching on the brown bag.

Stephanie remarked, "You are showing us that the capture of dominions is vital work."

Malcolm responded, "Yes, but remember its simplicity. There will be detailed information given during times of prayer, corporate prayer, prayer over cities and nations, intercessory prayer where the full use of these vital works of capturing dominions will be used. There will be great freedom, atmospheric changes, landscape changes, mass movement."

Stephanie said, "I'm seeing movement twofold—like a massive group of people moving and then the movement as an earthquake would bring to the shifting of land."

"This is no light matter, but it is simplistic. Heaven will instruct because the power of the blood and the final work of Jesus have created this for mankind. The groaning of the earth has called out for such a time as this."

The Mass Release of LHS's

Stephanie suddenly saw the book of Daniel in front of her briefly. It was a glimpse of the book of Daniel, and Wisdom was reminding us of our time with her when she said that things that were closed in the book of Daniel are being revealed. Stephanie explained, "I just keep seeing quick flashes of the use of the capture bags, but specifically I have a very far-reaching bird's-eye view. I'm way up in the sky and I'm looking at some ocean waterways and embankments. Some of what I see is on land, and when these capture bags are utilized, there is a freeing of LHS's that have been trapped. I'm seeing hundreds of them going up, and I know that they are LHS's."

I asked, "Is there a streamlining to that process for the mass release of LHS's?"

Malcolm replied, "It will be in the use of these (brown) capture bags of dominions. The evil dominions have held them and traded on them."

She then saw a visual of a massive angel with a capture bag. "He flew down with the bag and captured the dominion in it. Whereas before it appeared as if a dark film had been over the landscape, suddenly light came breaking through. It produced an atmospheric change that allowed the release of LHS's that have been in captivity because when you capture the dominion, you're not capturing the souls of people or the spirits of people, you are capturing the demonic principality."

She continued, "I'm still seeing this angel. What they are showing me is the simplicity that is the capture. The complexity is in knowing when and how to commission the angels."

Stephanie was seeing in detail a scene like what we experienced with the Sandhills Ecclesia as we did courtroom work concerning Mississippi and Canada. At that time David[30] saw a segment of the Mississippi River with LHS's coming out of it and going through the silver channel.

---

[30] David Porter III, Lead Apostle for Sandhills Ecclesia

Malcolm urged, "Taste and see that the Lord is good. More instruction will come. It will seem tedious at first, but it will become very natural to you to do this."

We could perceive that everyone we had seen was very well pleased. That's the word we got without them saying it. They are very well pleased. They are glad that this work is going to be done.

Stephanie saw many Warrior Angels outside the window of the conference room.

I asked, "Are these capturing angels?"

"Yes," was the reply, "They are part of this work. They are simply waiting to be deployed, and they are waiting with great anticipation."

A passage of Scripture came to mind from Romans 8:

[18] I am convinced that any suffering we endure is less than nothing compared to the magnitude of glory that is about to be unveiled within us. [19] The entire universe is standing on tiptoe, yearning to see the unveiling of God's glorious sons and daughters!

[20] For against its will, the universe itself has had to endure the empty futility resulting from the consequences of human sin. But now, with eager expectation, [21] all creation longs for freedom from its slavery to decay and to experience with us the wonderful freedom coming to God's children. [22] To this day we are aware of the universal agony and groaning of creation, as if it were in the

contractions of labor for childbirth. ^{23} And it's not just creation. We who have already experienced the first fruits of the Spirit also inwardly groan as we passionately long to experience our full status as God's sons and daughters—including our physical bodies being transformed.

^{24} For this is the hope of our salvation. But hope means that we must trust and wait for what is still unseen. For why would we need to hope for something we already have? ^{25} So because our hope is set on what is yet to be seen, we patiently keep on waiting for its fulfillment. (Romans 8: 18-25)

Stephanie commented, "What this brown capture bag unravels are those three things where our sin brought us into the captivity. That includes LHS and their activity."

We were in awe because we were seeing this ancient text played out now!

"Malcolm, is there anything else today?" we desired to know.

He answered, "Your obedience to release the LHS book instead of partner with fear has laid the foundation for this next level of revelation. The consequence of this will be the mass release of LHS's as people walk in this new revelation and co-labor with Heaven and with angels. There had to be a beginning."

Tan Capture Bags

Stephanie and I had engaged Heaven regarding more information on the capture bags. Ezekiel, who met us explained. "Do not assume the possibility that there is every color of bag available to do different things in the spirit. There are some we may not yet ever know what the color is, but the usefulness of the bags is available on behalf of the people's angels to have full use of. There are dynamics of the use of every bag, including the color of this one."

The bag he was holding looked like camel hair, a tan color. Stephanie remarked to Ezekiel, "You said the words 'camel hair,' and then you said, 'hairy.' It's funny how Heaven makes me do correlations of words based on other words, what does this hairy mean? I mean, how does that relate to the bags?" Stephanie then saw that **they use them in correlation with and in conjunction with the domain bags (orange bags) which are very specific to domains,** not in an inclusive way of just what we think of as domains within websites, but domains **of the enemy.**

Ezekiel said, "There is treachery in domains. There is heresy in domains."

Stephanie explained, "The way I'm seeing you use this is not necessarily in *capturing* anything. It is used by laying it down upon the treachery, upon the heresy that is in those domains, covering it. I saw the camel hair. It has what I know in the natural as having a weight to it.

Think of it as a trampling. You lay them down and you use them in that manner. The usefulness of it as a trampling upon the domains as you go and you capture domains, you lay it down, ahead of the treachery or on top of the treachery.[31] You lay it on the treachery and the heresy."

Stephanie remarked, "The heresy you're showing me as an actual, tangible thing. Not just a word or a deed, it looks like a tangibleness.

Ezekiel said, **"Heresies create structures. We trample down the heresy and the treachery with the use of this bag."**

Stephanie said, "I am seeing clearly how you are using this in a setting where occultism is involved."

Ezekiel explained, "The foundation of occultism is heresy. It is treachery."

Stephanie remarked, "I am seeing it so clearly, the bags provide a covering where your feet can land securely as you go into a place as a conquering. As we've read in the Bible where our feet tread upon the adder and the lion, and our feet tread upon the serpent and the snake. This is like that!

"Oh, you just showed me in the natural, when there's a snake, what we're supposed to do is throw a blanket over it or throw something over it and stomp on it. That

---

[31] Psalm 91:13, Luke 10:19

is what I just saw Ezekiel do! Ezekiel, can we commission you with these bags?"

Ezekiel reminded us that the understanding of these bags is for our purposes to know *what* they are conquering. It is a way in which we can understand how the commissioning can be done.

Stephanie asked, "Ezekiel, is there anything else that you need for today? Is there anything else you want to show us about this bag or commissioning's?

She began a commissioning,

We commission that these bags be laid out before you as you tread upon the lion and the adder, as you tread upon the scorpion and the snake, for these to be laid out before you as you co-labor. As you walk in the victories, THAT is the full use, Ezekiel.

Ezekiel, we commend you to the Father. You, your ranks, and your commanders, and we commission you, your commanders, and ranks with the full use of this bag, to lay it down before the people, to lay it down upon the treachery—upon the heresy. As we move forward, co-laboring with you, we can walk and tread upon the lion and the adder, to tread upon the scorpion and the snake; to tread upon those things with victory, commissioning you to do this in full use of all the other bags, in time and out of time and in every realm and dimension.

We seal this with the blood of Jesus and the Sword of the Lord. We thank you.

We thank you, Father, that you keep showing us how you go before us, preparing every way.

Describing what she was now seeing, Stephanie said, "I'm seeing Ezekiel snatching up things using black bags. I'm seeing him using the purple bags right now. He has laid down those bags before him. I'm watching him with domains, capturing with the orange bags. It's as if I'm seeing the way in which the enemy has put together, their use of infiltrations into domains using occultism and all of that together. This is just such a complete picture of that."

———·———

Chapter 12
Pink Capture Bags

Stephanie and I had engaged Heaven and we were in a boardroom with Malcolm. We had questions about some of the colors of bags others had seen and had asked me about.

Pink Capture Bags

On the whiteboard, Malcolm drew a pink bag and said, "It was for capturing innocence that has been stolen."

Stephanie asked, "How are they utilized where innocence has been stolen?"

He began, "This, too, is an in time and out of time revelation. Just as a newborn arrives with innocence, and the purity that is present within a newborn, there is still deep corruption in the DNA and RNA, even at birth, even though they appear innocent. That is why this is used in time and out of time. The innocence that was stolen in the generational line can be brought to bear."

"Can it then be restored to the person or to the family line?" Stephanie questioned.

Malcolm showed Stephanie innocence being brought back to the Kingdom of Heaven, into heavenly realms. She remarked, "As the angels bring the innocence that was stolen into the heavenly realms, as people step into Heaven, innocence will greet them." The vision was of innocence as a piece of themselves greeting them and enveloping them, restoring the innocence that was taken from them—from their RNA and from their DNA. It becomes as a covering upon their realms—like a garment.

Stephanie asked in her heart, "Why is this being given in Heaven?" and she heard the answer, "That is where innocence stands."

She asked, "Does that bring wholeness back to their soul or their spirit?"

"As a covering, yes," Malcolm disclosed.

Stephanie described the picture she had, "Someone steps into Heaven, and they have asked for this innocence to be brought back to them or to a family member. When they step into Heaven it is like they are greeted by it. I saw a greeting like 'Hello, Stephanie!' and an acknowledgement of 'Hello innocence.' It became like a garment. It was put on like a robe over the whole being."

I asked, "What's the procedure to use this for restoring innocence?"

Malcolm replied, "Repentance for the generational line for participating or being a part of the corruption that steals the innocence—the stolen innocence from the ages."

Stephanie interjected, "My question is this, if it is our spirit man in Heaven and innocence greets us there, this is the truest understanding of living spirit forward. Your spirit man wears innocence as a garment and brings it to the soul and to the body. Is that right? That is how I am seeing this play out because I am still seeing it as a greeting in Heaven. It is a calling of it back to yourself. With the understanding that because of the finished work, the complete work, that Jesus did, we can call back the innocence of our RNA and DNA. We can bring it from our spirit man to our soul, then it comes to the body. It is a co-laboring of our spirit man and our soul and our body, too. They are showing me how Heaven has perfected what co-laboring means. They have been showing us over the last while the co-laboring of the angels with us. Recently, they have shown us the co-laboring that will be between us and each other as we walk through this. Now they are showing us the co-laboring of our spirit, soul, and body."

"This is a labor of love from the Father," Malcom stated.

Stephanie observed, "When I saw the word 'labor,' I saw it as a woman in labor giving birth to the next generation where even though they are innocent (there is such innocence with a newborn) yet there is still such corruption already present from the generational lines."

Stephanie said, "May I ask a question? In doing this on behalf of our generations, as we do this work with Freemasonry, Mithraism, and other things, with calling this innocence back to ourselves, how will this affect the next generation?"

He responded, "This is part of the work—the finished work. As you walk through the realms of Heaven, you can do this on behalf of people with the authority that you carry."

She asked, "Are you showing me that we can stir up someone's spirit man that is asleep?"

He confirmed, "That is a simple way to put it. All the downloads from Heaven from the Godly bonds that are released upon people's realms is, in fact, a stirring up of spirits who are asleep. Have you not seen the evidence of that?"

"I have," Stephanie acknowledged.

Then she said, "The picture I have in front of me is of intercessors. (We *are* intercessors when we pray on behalf of our families and those in our families that are asleep.) We have been releasing Godly bonds for them, and it has awakened their spirits. This is the same principle."

I asked, "What are earmarks of the loss of innocence in people?"

He replied, "Their DNA?"

Stephanie asked, "Are you saying the simple fact that we're born?"

"Yes," he emphasized. "That is the number one ear marker. All of your innocence has been stolen in some way."

Malcolm responded, "The heart of the Father is to continually be restoring humanity back into Himself. The tools, this revelation, these are taking away the hindrances that have been upon the hearts and minds through the spirit of religion. These are effective. They are effective in intercessory work. They are effective when you pray for your family. Use these effectively. Remember the color of the bags is for your understanding of what you can capture or what you can release. It is just one of the tools.

"Now you have seen two capture bags that are in time and out of time—purple and pink—and as you are doing this work, you may see where pink is utilized."

Stephanie decided, "Well, I am going to do this now.

I call my angels near. I call Ezekiel, his commanders, and his ranks near. I am requesting that you, in the name of Jesus, use the pink bags to capture and bring back from the very beginning—from the hand of the Father to now—the innocence that has been stolen throughout the generations. I repent on behalf of my generations for agreeing with the enemy that took away and

> *stole the innocence all the way back to the garden, and that corrupted my DNA and RNA. I request that this be brought back to my realms for my spirit in the name of Jesus.*

Stephanie described what was happening, "I'm being handed a garment and it's a garment of innocence. I'm going to put it on, and I am going to speak to my soul, 'Soul, do not be a gatekeeper. Accept this garment of innocence. It has been given as a gift from the Father. Body, accept this garment of innocence as it begins to reconstruct my DNA and RNA, in Jesus' name.'"

We then decided to do the same for a friend we shall call Robin. Stephanie said,

> *I call Robin's angels near to co-labor with Ezekiel, his commanders, and ranks with my angels, and commission you to go back in time and out of time on behalf of Robin, as we repent on behalf of the generations for partnering with and for being a part of the innocence stolen that has affected the DNA and the RNA all the way back to the hand of the Father.*
>
> *We commission you to bring back the innocence that has been stolen.*
>
> *I call Robin's spirit into heavenly realms to have the garment of innocence placed upon her and I speak to Robin's spirit to teach the soul not to be a gatekeeper and to bring it into her body, to change her DNA and RNA back to the innocence*

that the Father designed in His original plan for us, in Jesus' name.

Malcolm said, "Aren't you glad that innocence can be brought back to the body? Many people will struggle with this concept because they have divulged themselves into false understanding that the Father cannot restore innocence that has been stolen. This goes to that Scripture where they believe in godliness, but not the power of it."[32]

I was reminded of a testimony I heard of a woman who had been a prostitute. She got born again and it was important to her to have her innocence restored. She just cried to the Lord for that. Sometime later, she ended up getting remarried and on her wedding night, her sheets were bloody. Her innocence had been restored.

We talked a few moments of how important this is for children whose innocence was stolen by others, for those who have been involved in sex trafficking or similar things. Having innocence restored can go a long way to wholeness for them, and Heaven has obliged us with a simple way to see innocence restored.

Malcolm reminded us that even though we do not have a full understanding of how this works, it is all done in the spirit realm.

---

[32] 2 Timothy 3:5

Stephanie said, "I accept all that Heaven has. I was just trying to get clarification on how this was the only bag that was used as you step into Heaven."

Malcolm replied, "It's because of the purity there. That is where the innocence is put upon you, and it is brought into your realms."

The Angel Purity

I asked, "Would there be a co-laboring with the Angel Purity?"

As soon as I said that the Angel Purity appeared. Stephanie had never met her, but Purity said to her, "But I've met you."

Stephanie described her as I had seen her. The essence of her being was purity. She looks like her name.

Purity said, "I have longed with the heart of the Father regarding innocence for people—innocence and purity."

Stephanie explained, "She just showed it to me like they live in the same house together. That they are one. This is what the completion of this work is—that they are one.

"Purity, you are the final piece of this puzzle, aren't you?"

Purity replied affirmatively.

Stephanie continued,

As an act of faith, when we step into Heaven, and we ask for the innocence to be brought back to us and we are robed with it. Purity's job, the work that she will do as we bring that to our realms, to our spirit, soul, and body, is the knitting together of our being.

I commission you, Purity, to take my garment of innocence that I have received in Heaven and to knit them to my soul and to my body, in Jesus' name.

And I commission you to work with my friend Robin, to knit together for her the garment of innocence and to knit it with her soul and her body.

Purity remarked, "This is part of the redeeming."

I remarked about something I had learned from Joseph Sturgeon,[33] that Purity had worked with Noah when it was said, "He was made perfect in his generations."[34] Purity worked with Noah and his DNA to remove the spots.

Purity said, "Because he stepped into Heaven and received his innocence, because he forgave his ancestors (Noah understood iniquity in the generations because the Lord had revealed that to him), he did what looked like courtroom work on behalf of his generations. This

---

[33] *Treasures of Darkness, Volume 2: Echoes of a Father* by Joseph Sturgeon, Feline Graphics (2016)
[34] Genesis 6:9

was part of the restoration of his innocence and the restoration of his DNA and RNA."

Stephanie then saw a picture of Moses where he was up on the mountain, and as he is coming down his face shone so brightly that they had to cover his face. Purity explained that the only reason it happened in the natural is because there was restoration to his soul and his body of the innocence that had been stolen, which in turn brought the knitting of that innocence to his soul and his body because of her work.

---
*When there is innocence
there is purity.*

Stephanie realized, "That is why you are showing me that they all live in the same house together. They are one in that sense, because without corruption, when there's true innocence the way the Father created us to be, there is purity."

Purity then showed how Eve, even though she was deceived and ate of the fruit, lost her purity. She still had innocence, but Adam lost both at the same time when he ate of the fruit. In a sense, innocence is something we wear. That is why it can be easily discarded when we sin, but it is also how it is corrupted in generations.

Stephanie ended by saying, "Now, I've come back full circle and Malcolm is standing there at the whiteboard with the same giant bag that he drew in pink, and he's just smiling with his chalk in his hand."

Capture Bag Commission

Now that you have read about the various capture bags, I thought it would be appropriate to provide a template for commissioning your angels regarding the use of capture bags.

I call the angels assigned to me to come near.

Father, I request on behalf of these angels, all the different sizes, classifications, and colors of every capture bag needed to serve the Kingdom of Heaven and to serve your people in Jesus' name.

I commission the angels assigned to me to use every classification, size, and color of capturing bag needed; to go and capture the infiltrations; to use the different colors and classifications of the bags as needed from the smallest demon to the largest domain, in the name of Jesus; to use these capturing bags throughout my realms and those of my family.

I commission you to network and cooperate with Ezekiel, his commanders, and ranks and to work with the Bond Registry angels, in Jesus' name.

Chapter 13
Rough Places in the Road

Malcolm asked, "Would you like to know about the rough places in the road?"

We replied, "Yes, sir."

Stephanie began, "As I'm seeing this play out, it's as if a car is on the road, and they hit a pothole—a rough place—and it damages the tire. Even though you don't realize that there have been small, minor increments of damage to the tire—there has been, and it wears away over time."

Malcolm responded, "It's the same as the wearing away of the soul. The usefulness of these tools will lessen the rough patches in the road. The usefulness of these tools will also lessen how the soul gets weary and tired of the day in, and day out struggles, misconceptions, and untidiness of life. These tools are for the sons of God."

Stephanie noted, "I'm just standing here looking at the rough patches in the road and watching it become a smooth path. As we use this dynamic, it is like watching new pavement develop."

We thanked Malcolm saying, "We'll be back for more."

As this engagement was ending, he handed Stephanie a blue capture bag on the way out. Stephanie explained, "In that split second moment when he handed me that blue bag (of course I commissioned my angels for the use of it), an understanding and a knowing came that if we see in the spirit, if we are in the spirit, if we are praying and we see a blue capture bag it is an understanding that the enemy is going to be coming with accusations that can be dismantled easily."

Thank you, Father!

The Ballroom

This engagement with Heaven started out with an interesting scene. We were in a large golden ballroom with large giant balls bouncing around with people inside them. They were like the Human Hamster Balls that you can get inside and roll around without getting hurt. Malcolm was present and laughing at the sight. We, of course, had questions.

Malcolm said, "Would you like another Lesson in Leaning?" (This time spelled 'leaning' instead of 'liening' as we had seen in prior engagements and as if we were leaning upon each other.) He expounded, "The concept of these bouncing balls is profound, yet simplistic. Many in the Body of Christ feel like they have been bouncing around from one place to another; from one ministry to another; from one hopelessness to another; or from one flavor of understanding after another."

"Malcolm, are you talking about other religions?" Stephanie asked.

"Yes," he confirmed, "people have been searching. Some have been pining away in the dark, not knowing where to go."

Stephanie asked, "Why are you showing me these bouncing balls in this ballroom?"

He responded, "Because they look like fun and are in a place that is safe, like the balls are not going to run away. They are not going to run out into the street. The people are in a place that feels free, but also secure."

Suddenly, all the balls just stopped and fell to the ground and Malcolm turned toward Stephanie, saying, "This is what people have been seeking for, a place where they find freedom and a place of security. This is the Father's Kingdom. That is Kingdom Dynamics. These balls represent people. The Father's heart is that they are not bouncing around in the world from one place to another, but their hearts and minds are free in the Father's Kingdom to bounce things off one another, to be at play in their heart and in their minds with one another.

"Do you see joy and the fun of these bouncing balls? What the Father is bringing to the body will bring this joy, this freedom, and this security. There is security and secureness in Him, and He will bring it to each of you. Then you will show one another this freedom and this security. People will see it. They will feel it. They will hear it. They will understand it from one another."

Stephanie commented, "Now he is showing me all different colors. All the balls change colors. This represents different nationalities, different colors of people yet in this room. We are in unison. We are in unity. We are in security. Malcolm, with this lesson on leaning, what is the lesson here? Can you make it clear to us?"

Malcolm responded, "The lesson here is trust of trust. It is how people will experience the trust of trust. They will trust the Father. They will trust this Kingdom Dynamic. There will be security in it. They will feel it."

Stephanie reflected, "I don't know that very many people have experienced that kind of security with other people within a ministry, but you are showing me that that's what this will be? That that's what this is—freedom, unity, security in the Father's Kingdom." She quietly said, "But why in a ballroom?"

He answered, "Well, where else would balls be?"

"It is because I choose to come in as a little child. Dr. Ron chooses to come in as a child," Stephanie stated.

Malcolm turned and said, "I much enjoy this."

Being Entrusted

The scenery then changed, and we found ourselves in the boardroom. Wisdom was present. She stepped forward to where we were sitting at the conference table, and she called us by name saying, "Stephanie and Ron, because you have chosen to invoke me in this work and on behalf of the Body of Christ, you have told the body the value that Wisdom brings to the table. There is an extension to the provision that is Wisdom. When you are trusted, you will be *entrusted*. There is more, so much more that the Kingdom of Heaven is bringing to light. It is also a part of the *trust of trust* that you are walking in with the Father and the Kingdom of Heaven. Expect more! Expect greater! Expect!

———·———

Chapter 14
Unweaving Domains

As Stephanie and I engaged this day, we were taken to a conference room where we were seated. On the table in the room was a map. It appeared that the entire table was a map. A man in white linen named Timothy was also with us. We had met with him on a prior occasion. He informed us that he was from the Strategy Room. We could see what looked like stitching on the map that delineated one area from another like you see on a map showing the border of states or countries.

Stephanie inquired, "Can you tell me what I'm seeing Timothy?"

He informed us that the stitching was the border between domains.

He said, "This will go along with the Lessons on Liening."

I asked if he would define domain for us.

He replied, "This domain is different than an internet domain. This is like a territory, but you must consider it a domain."

The view of the map changed to a broader view. It was not of anyplace identifiable to us. It was just for the purpose of understanding.

He continued, "The stitching that you see is a weaving—an intertwining of domains which is corruption upon the land and how we see territories. Territories can be in the natural and they are in the spirit as well. In the supernatural, the wicked want territory. They despise losing territory. We need to undo the weaving."

Stephanie replied, "Okay, Timothy, how do we do that?"

Timothy said, "I'm present because these strategies come from the Strategy Room. We can detect and see the domains, the stitching, and the weaving of the territories from the enemy. This is upon the territories of people's realms, their hearts, and their minds. The Lessons in Lienings will obstruct the enemy from the weaving as you walk in this prayer paradigm."

Stephanie responded saying, "Okay, so Malcolm (who had appeared in the room) and Timothy, are you saying that this is the next part of learning about liening, and capturing bags,[35] because I see that we must use the

---

[35] These will be described in an upcoming chapter.

capturing bags in equipping our angels for capturing domains. Is this part of that?"

Malcolm replied, "Yes. Remember you are a region. Realms are territories. Principalities are over regions and territories. That's what you have learned in the natural. Now you're learning that it is also spiritual within realms of a person, so let's undo the weaving."

"How do we do that? Stephanie asked.

Malcolm replied, "In your lessons on leaning, you learned about parameters. This is a parameter—this weaving, this domain captured from the enemy."

Stephanie remarked, "Okay. I do see it, Malcolm, as an actual capture."

She then explained to me what she was seeing, "Dr. Ron, the way I am seeing this is—on one side I saw what would be considered the land mass on the map, then I saw the stitching between the domains and that the enemy had control of this. He had weaved himself into another piece of territory, and that weaving together has created a bond, a stitching together. It is not like a tether or a soul tie. It is a weaving together."

Malcolm continued, "Remember what you learned about Lessons on Liening where you deal with the consequential liens in the Court of Cancellations. It will be just as easy to undo the weaving in that same court."

Stephanie asked, "Malcolm, are you saying this is another step?"

"No," he replied, "this is part of the same. It's just a clearer understanding."

He continued, "Let's undo the weaving. Okay?"

He explained, "The weaving is a condition that has been placed upon the lien."

She asked, "What is the condition that permitted this?"

He replied, "It is bloodshed. That is the trade that allows the principality to weave this territory to another."

She asked, "Are you talking about generationally?"

"Yes," he replied.

Stephanie commented, "What you're saying is for our understanding, and the purposes of understanding how to implement this in our everyday work, is that it was the generational line that made the sacrifice upon the land, because it was upon a land mass in the natural, that empowered a principality into the generational line because of the parameters put upon the trust. It created a stitching between the generations. That's why it has come down generation after generation after generation. That is how it has been able to do it in time and at of time, is this correct Malcolm?"

He said, "Yes, that is the correct understanding. People will question, 'How has a principality been able to follow a generational line?' The DNA is corrupted. This blood sacrifice that allowed the condition for the principality created the generational weaving from one generation to the next, the trade that was made has allowed that principality to follow the generations down the line. Let's undo the weaving."

Stephanie asked, "How do we undo the weaving in the Court of Cancellations?"

He replied, "After the repentance work on behalf of the generations in the Court of Cancellations, as you cancel every covenant, oath, vow, bloodshed and the impact of that, and the angels strike the parameters, you commission them to use the capture bags in time and out of time. This will undo the weaving in the generations. It's an unstitching. It's an overturning. It's an undoing and the finished work (of Jesus) will be complete because the finished work is complete."

Recognizing that Stephanie's soul was struggling to comprehend this information, Malcolm said to her, "I give you ease Stephanie." He added, "The ease of this flow will come to all that work in this."

She replied, "Thank you for that, Malcolm. That's good to know."

She observed, "Timothy[36] is quite pleased with the work that had been done earlier in the Strategy Rooms; it has created a buzz."

---

[36] Timothy is a man in white linen who assisted us.

Timothy affirmed, "It has created a buzz in the Strategy Room from the excitement for all that is coming and for all of the good work that is being done."

Describing what she was seeing, she said, "I can see them celebrating the fact that the angels are utilizing the strategies and the capturing bags and are co-laboring with us as we are doing this paradigm work with the Courts of Heaven and how much of an impact it is going to have upon lives of people. They are excited about all of this."

Stephanie realized the map was still in front of her, so she paused and asked what was next.

Ezekiel, who was now present, desired a commissioning. Stephanie began,

> *Ezekiel, I commission you, your commanders, and your ranks to undo the weaving on behalf of LifeSpring International Ministries, Sandhills Ecclesia, CourtsNet, Heaven Down Business, and the other ministries, as well as for every employee and their families, in the name of Jesus.*
>
> *I request of the Father a Garment of Ease. I request that a Garment of Ease be given to every person on the ministry team, and those that have purchased this book, or attended one of our conferences for this new revelation that Heaven has brought.*

Ezekiel, we commission you to administer this garment of ease for this revelation on behalf of the Kingdom of Heaven, in Jesus' name.

Ezekiel then placed a Garment of Ease on both of us and we watched as he went to his commanders and ranks to begin instructing them about the Garments of Ease and the capturing bags he had in his hands. Stephanie was amazed at the vast number of ranks of angels gathered.

We thanked Malcolm and Timothy for their assistance. Timothy said, "I am leaving this map on this table because we will be seeing it again."

———·———

Chapter 15
The Banners of the Lord

As we engaged Heaven at this time, the room was suddenly filled with Angels. Ezekiel appeared and we asked, "Is there a commissioning that you need?"

Stephanie heard in her spirit a commissioning, so she began,

> *I commission you Ezekiel, your commanders, and your ranks to break the standard of old. To remove its powers, its frequencies, its hindrances, its telecommunications, its systems. Do this by use of every capturing bag, in time and out of time and in every dimension and take it and destroy it in the name of Jesus. Use the armaments of Heaven and the weaponry of Heaven. Use your good skill, in Jesus' name.*
>
> *I commission you to remove any old banners that you see and replace the old banner with the Banner of the Lord. To stake it, mark it, and highlight it, in Jesus' name!*

The angels were all still standing with us, so apparently, we were not finished. Stephanie added,

Father, I ask on all their behalf, angel food, bread, and elixir.

She noted, "Now they're leaving."

The lights in the room dimmed and a movie began playing on the screen that had appeared. Everyone in the room was watching a movie of some angelic activity. One could see a variety of landscapes. Some with cities and town. One could see a mapping of people's minds. Scattered about the landscape, the angels were planting red flags (banners) where the territories had been reclaimed and restored. The flags were on tall poles so the enemy could see that this was territory that had been taken and given back to the Kingdom of Heaven, because of the blood, because of the commissioning, because of the co-laboring, because of the obedience. The movie explained all this as the reason this movement is taking place.

Stephanie commented, "Lydia and Malcolm, when you say movement, there's a double meaning. I see the movement of when the earth moves under the force of an earthquake as it realigns itself and shifts. I also see a movement, as in the Body of Christ, coming together and moving in unison. Its march step is in unison. When they stake these banners in the ground, initially the ground is barren, and then, it turns lush after the banner is staked in the ground. There is an enumerable number of angels doing this work. That's why it was so crowded in the room. They were pressed up almost against me.

Malcolm said, "Taste and see that the Lord is good."

Stephanie continued, "I'm watching Malcom and Lydia be in awe and wonder and joy of what this movie is showing."

She asked, "Malcom, Lydia, is this a result of the new revelation or of the Kingdom Dynamics of Heaven and all that we have learned?"

Malcom said, "It is because we choose the Kingdom of Heaven. We choose the co-laboring. We choose the partnership. We choose the love of our Savior and of our Father. This is a direct result of all those things. This is Kingdom Dynamics."

Stephanie said, "Dr. Ron, I'm seeing land and I'm also seeing people's minds that were barren and ugly, like scorched earth becoming lush green with rich colors. Angels are really planting these banners high. What is significant, is that I don't view it or see it as we would see these banners. It is like how they used to capture kingdoms and they would put the new flag up. That's what this is. Capturing of dominions, capturing domains, and overturning the principalities is exactly that. It's putting up the new flag. Thank you, Father."

The movie ended and they turned the lights back on in the room.

Wisdom came in and said, "I'm pleased with the revelation that's been revealed and is being utilized because of the importance of it, because we are dealing with principalities." She reiterated to us the importance of us utilizing her in every scenario and situation when it comes to that work. She gave Stephanie a big pearl, much larger than the one she had been given on a prior engagement. With that, Wisdom went and stood along the wall.

The red flags were not for us to see. It was for the enemy to see that territory had been taken back.

Jesus was also in the room now, and the room was filled with His love. It enveloped the room because the people have been freed of the domination of the dominion. They will begin to experience His love. Relational freedom will be found by people in this as the banners are being raised and the flags are being turned back to Jesus and as the territories are returned to Him when the stakes are placed in the ground.

The day prior, Stephanie and I had engaged Heaven and were taught about the red banners and the Banner of the Lord. This day, as we stepped in, we could see Ezekiel waving a red flag for the Conquering King—Jesus.

We asked, "Ezekiel, what can you tell us about this?"

We were in a conference room and Ezekiel was pleased to have the red flag that he was waving. He stated, "There are many things being accomplished in the spirit through the revelation and the co-laboring but there is much more to be done. This is Heaven's way of sharing that the Conquering King has conquered, and as you already know, things have been conquered." Ezekiel continued, "We talk about how the Conquering King has conquered, but so many people live their lives with things going well, but for others it seems like things are not feeling very conquered, right? The demonstration in this room today shows that there are specific things that the Conquering King has conquered based on the prayer paradigms and the co-laboring with the angels that these things have been taking place. It is an assurance."

Ezekiel then took the red banner and staked it in the ground.

We asked, "Was this a dominion that you conquered?"

He stated, "This was places that I conquered." We asked if he could be more specific and Stephanie began seeing a prior vision where all the angels were going out, planting the flags, but this time they were being planted on the map of the brain. He clarified, "We are taking back fresh territory, where the King has taken back new territory of mindsets."

As she watched, a video played out in front of her of the same vision of the angels taking territory back. It was a lot of different angels, and they were conquering separate places in the brain.

We asked, "Ezekiel, this would be the satisfaction of consequential liens upon people's lives that even change their thinking, because you are showing me this brain that was like scorched earth?"

He replied, "Yes. Thought processes, synapses, intelligence, or the perception of someone's intelligence within themselves, redeemed by the Blood of the Lamb, redeemed by the Conquering King."

We then inquired, "Is there anything that you need, or your commanders and ranks want or desire?" Immediately Ezekiel said, "'Commissionings.' We have been waiting for these times, for this age, for this co-laboring."

We asked, "What commissioning?"

He answered, "From the simplest commissioning to the greatest, that it is their joy and honor to do for the King."

"What is the commissioning today, Ezekiel?"

Stephanie was reminded of a commissioning she gave during a session with a client:

> *Based on the knowledge that, because of Father's calling to the sons to act to forgive as John 20:23 instructs us, and based on Romans 8:33 stating that God is the Judge who has issued HIS final verdict over them of not guilty—we commission the innumerable warring and capture angels who, have been called for such a time as this, to be released this minute, in time and out of time and*

in every dimension, using the full resources of Heaven, HIS Kingdom, HIS authority, to war on behalf of the peoples to bring about the swift changes meant for and on behalf of the land, this nation, the people, the minds, and the hearts. To take the bounty that are the princes—to remove them and their ranks under them, to capture the dominion and the domain, the kingdom, the structures, the iron gates, the foundations—and to take the plunder that belongs to THE Kingdom of Heaven and His sons. To take the broken standards of old, and to break them and burn them. Then we request from the Court of Titles and Deeds, that ownership be given back to King Jesus.

This commission went to Ezekiel, his commanders, and his ranks to do that work.

Ezekiel charged us, "Remind the peoples that are associated with LifeSpring International Ministries, those on Tuesday night, the Platinum Members, those that trade with LifeSpring, that because of that trade, those that trade with LifeSpring have full utilization to have their angels link arms with his ranks and commanders. The commissions have been great. The peoples have been using these commissions to draw upon this knowledge and understanding and to use it to their advantage. It is for their advantage. It is a gift from the King. The utilization of angel armies is a gift. They are well-equipped to do this on behalf of the sons, and they await with great anticipation every time we do it—there is a joint co-laboring, I mean."

Stephanie remarked, "I was seeing it a little bit one sided before, where we were doing the commissioning and they were doing all the work and that is true. However, what he was just telling me was that they enjoy the co-laboring, and they enjoy coming alongside and helping us to know how to commission them and what to say—that it is a dual thing."

"Thank you," we responded, "Ezekiel, we enjoy the relationship too."

He answered, "Yes, this is relational. It is profound."

We next inquired, "What is the commission you would like from us today?"

As soon as we quizzed him about this, a lot of angels came in the room. These were higher ranking angels. These were his commanders. On the table, the map we had seen before presented itself in front of us on the table. Ezekiel began showing us that some of the commanders, their specific job is undoing the weaving. For other commanders, their specific jobs are capture bags. Some were going to release other angels. There were specific jobs for each of the commanders.

We understood that concept, but Ezekiel wanted us to understand the force behind this concept of co-laboring with angels, that a force to be reckoned with that has been laid upon the foundations of LifeSpring because of the understanding of co-laboring. He reminded us of when Donna saw the number of angels grow in number and that they continue to do that.

We requested, "Would you help us with the commissioning?"

> *Ezekiel, we commission you, your commanders and ranks to the undoing of territories and joined land masses and domains, as necessary.*
>
> *We request of the Father capture bags of every size and color and purpose to be released to them and we commission them for the full use of those capture bags based upon their purpose. We release you to do that.*
>
> *We commission you for releasing understanding to the people that are joined with us in the ministry. We commission you to those to fund the various aspects of the ministry and to bring favor for those working on behalf of the ministry.*
>
> *Father, I am requesting on their behalf golden lassos. We commission you, Ezekiel, to use the golden lassos and take what would have been the frequencies of a storm and collapse them right before our feet.*
>
> *I commission your angels that are specified to the unweaving to undo the weaving in the mighty name of Jesus.*
>
> *Father, we ask for more encampments on behalf of Ezekiel. We thank you, Father. Thank You for*

the growth. It is a gift from You, Father. We thank You for that.

I commission you, Ezekiel, to take the banner of the Lord and the poles and stake in the ground with the red flag on behalf of the ministry and all aspects of it, in Jesus' name.

We commission you to collapse every storm, use fog dispeller as necessary, and utilize every weaponry at your disposal on behalf of the ministry, those who are part of the team, and those connected to the ministry in any fashion, in Jesus' name.

Ezekiel began instructing the commanders now in the room, then they saluted him and filed out of the room. Ezekiel stepped aside awaiting the next person to speak.

The Personal Guarantee

Lydia, Malcolm, George, and Wisdom were in the room. George came forth holding a piece of paper in his hand—a document that he had signed. He explained the paper to us, "It is a Personal Guarantee of the Father for funds for the processes, plans, and purposes of Heaven having the backing of a personal guarantee by the Father of _everything_ being fully funded. He wanted this to be on record for all."

We thanked George and took the copy he gave us, as he kept a copy to put on file for us.

---

*He reminded us that
every assignment from Heaven
is fully funded.*

Wisdom at the Table

Wisdom took a seat at the table. Normally she stands. She began showing Stephanie how Wisdom grows within the hearts of men as we utilize her.

Stephanie described, "I am seeing it as a strength and as a literal growth within the person's spirit and soul. Every time we call upon her and invoke her in a situation, Wisdom grows inside of us, inside of our realms, inside of our hearts and our minds. As we gain more and more understanding from her, the relationship builds and grows. We always have a seat at the table with her (which is why she sat down)."

Stephanie responded, "Thank you for that Wisdom. I have so enjoyed this building of this relationship."

Stephanie described, "Just as the Father says, 'I am always with you,' Wisdom is showing it to me like the Father has taken a piece of Himself—a piece out of Himself and that is who she is. Of course, we know that Wisdom is one of the Seven Spirits of God, and she wants people to see this as a picture to understand that she is a true entity within the deity, that she can grow and build inside of each person that invokes her, that calls upon her, that walks with her, that holds her hand, that utilizes her in every situation. I see it as it being an internal strength, it becomes like steel inside of somebody, unwavering, unmoved, full understanding and knowledge come with that growth. She is showing me the rest of the Spirits of God, how they are. It is like a steely position within somebody. I am seeing it as iron inside of someone. Picture the guy named Wolverine in the X-Men movies. This is like that inside, but it is inside the whole body (not just the hands) and is like that kind of material. This is so our minds can understand how strong it is."

Wisdom reached over, grabbed Stephanie's hand, squeezed it, and got up from the table. Stephanie reacted with, "Thank you for that, Wisdom."

Stephanie mused, "It is good to know, because I have asked the question of how Understanding and Knowledge that I see as entities come alongside to work with us. Wisdom is showing me that as we grow with her, the other attributes of the Seven Spirits of God, Knowledge, Council, Understanding, Might, etc. come alongside us as well"

———·———

Chapter 16
Malcolm's Instruction

Malcolm came forward with chalk in his hand and went to the window that looked outside the room.

Stephanie paused to describe the boardroom we were in. She said, "When you come through the door, the head of one side of the table is right in front of you. Typically, we walk around behind it, and we sit, so we are in the middle of where the length of the table would be. There are still the two heads. Typically, across from us is a big door that people come in and out but sometimes they just come through the wall. To our left has always been a window and I have not typically seen things except light come through that window. Of course, the other day I saw angels standing on the other side of that window."

Malcolm began, "You see how with the pane of this window, you can see all the way through it to the other side. That is what this concept, this paradigm, this understanding is going to bring for people. They are going to be able to see to the other side, to the end of the road, to see the light at the end of the tunnel. It is an understanding that there is an end to the suffering here on earth. There can be a vision on the other side of the window that is new and all-encompassing of God's glory and favor. It is powerful. They can walk in it. They can live in it, and if they can see that, Hope arises."

He paused and drew a picture of a ledge, on the window.

Stephanie said, "I can see where there are people that feel like they are standing on the end of the ledge, treacherously either about to jump or fall off. Why are you showing me that, Malcolm?"

At that moment I had to take a short break and while on the break two people called the ministry expressing how desperate their situation was to them. They were on the edge.

She said, "Malcolm, I just saw this picture with the desperation that people have."

He said, "People are running to this ministry."

Stephanie was seeing a visual of people running to the ministry and because of our obedience, because of our trust of trust, because of our trust of ministry with its platform, the agreements with Heaven, the obedience of people, others will be able to see through this glass window to the other side to the Hope. Seeing through this glass, they will see not only the Hope of His calling but the Hope that you truly can live free in this life, free in your realms.

"Thank you, Malcolm," we replied.

He erased what Stephanie had been seeing, what he had drawn which was the ledge and people on it about to fall off. Stephanie said, "Now, I can see clearly through this window and there's great light shining through, peace shining through."

Malcolm continued, "The ebb and flow of this and what this will bring to people is the ebb and flow of the peace and the journey, and the peace and the journey. Instead of what we used to know as the ebb and flow as the storm, then the peace, then the journey, then the storm again."

Stephanie said, "This goes back to what you were talking about through consequential liens and the dynamics of this with no longer having the storms—just the peace and the journey."

As she was watching Malcolm, he erased the storm. On the glass was immediately that original picture of the little, tiny boat in the storm. Malcolm just started erasing the glass he used as a whiteboard.

Stephanie exclaimed, "That is glorious news, Malcolm!"

He said, "Because of the gloriousness of our Father, His reigning love is supreme. It just is. He wants this for his people now—for his people here alive now on the earth. The concept of gaining this after death is a misconception. It for now, and this is one of the ways. This ministry is leading the way. This ministry is a part of the way to this end."

Stephanie remarked, "When he showed me that 'this end.' I saw the window again, and the light on the other side—the light at the end of the tunnel—the breakthrough."

A Change of Ministry Procedures

I interrupted with a question, "Malcolm, should we redefine how we have been doing sessions? Should we start with the question, 'Are we looking at a consequential lien?' in our sessions?"

To clarify, we asked, "Is this additional understanding our starting point?"

"It is the ledge—the jumping off point," Malcolm answered.

"The Bond Registry is very necessary work," Malcom acknowledged. "It still will be there. It is still part of the completion, but start with, 'Is there a consequential lien?' The starting point, the jumping point is that question. The dismantling of many things through that process will have the Bond Registry work come with great ease. It is the simplification. It is the drilling down of this work.

"Remember K-I-S-S. Keep it simple, silly. Remember the shoelaces."

Stephanie explained, "He is showing me that even though we have a 90-minute timeframe, that even much more will be accomplished during that time. Because dealing with the consequential liens, the ungodly trusts and the removal of princes will make for easier work on behalf of the peoples in this paradigm."

"I have a question for you, Malcolm. When I am looking at an ungodly trust, is that going to be in the Guest Registry?" I inquired.

He replied, "It is on the Bond Registry. You will see it as a tab on the Personal or Family page. Move the tab to the front."

Stephanie interjected, "When we were first looking at this, he showed me a Post-it Note behind the Personal page on the Bond Registry."

Malcolm said, "Move the tab to the front of the page."

"Okay. That is easy. Thank you," we remarked.

Stephanie said, "He is still showing it to me as a small Post-it Note. The reason is because we try to make things bigger than what they are."

---
*It is **just** a principality!*

Stephanie laughed and commented, "I cannot believe that came out of my mouth because it was from Him!

"It *is* just a principality."[37]

Malcolm showed Stephanie how we have made this principality thought process so much bigger than it has to be.

I asked, "Malcolm, they can look at the Bond Registry and if they see the tab, they know they are dealing with a consequential lien, but start at the consequential lien?"

He replied, "Yes. If you see the tab, move the tab forward, then deal with that.

The consequential lien will lead us to an ungodly trust.

The consequential lien means there has been an ungodly trust established with a prince over it.

Stephanie explained, "He told us there is a difference between the ones with the parameter and ones outside of parameters."

Malcolm added, "The consequential lien that is outside the parameters is the one with a prince. The ones

---

[37] The tendency of the soul is to engage fear when we think of the overthrow of a principality. As sons we must choose to not cooperate with fear *at any* time *on any* level about *ANYTHING!* Have fearless faith!

inside the parameters have less strength. Almost all have a generational component. All are easily dealt with.

> *The consequential lien that is outside the parameters is the one with a prince. The ones inside the parameters have less strength.*

I said, "Malcolm, I am trying to get this as simple as I can for the Senior Advocates and Junior Advocates who will run with it, but they will have questions. We are just trying to filter questions.

"We know when we see a prince, we look for, 'What is the reason? What opened the door?' Then we repent accordingly. Is that right, Malcolm?"

He replied, "That is good process."

Stephanie remarked, "I will tell you the last two days, I have been in sessions with Karee and with Kevin. That is the way it worked out every single time. Then, if you go back and listen to Kevin's Sunday and Tuesday teaching, he does it exactly like that.

- "He saw the consequential lien,
- Then he saw the ungodly trust under it.
- He saw the parameters next.
- Under that, he saw the repentance work that takes care of the principality that has been ruling and governing over the ungodly trust with the parameters.

- **This is when it is struck—when it is removed."**

"Okay, Malcolm, what should we ask you?" I asked.

He said, "Ask me about the K-I-S-S."

"Okay, we are asking of you about keeping it simple."

Malcolm then put up the diagram of the parentheses. He turned around and said, "This is an example." He wrote inside of the parentheses the word 'smitten.'

He said,

Ungodly trusts create the parameter that is the consequential lien.

Stephanie inquired, "Inside that parameter is the consequential lien, and you wrote the word 'smitten' as an example?"

He said, "Yes."

She continued, "Then we know there is an ungodly trust?"

"Yes," he replied.

"You showed me that the next step is to ask, 'What is the ungodly trust? Is it an ungodly trust of trust? Is it an ungodly trust of friendship, ministry, et cetera? [we were to go down the list he gave us]."

"Yes. You will find the consequential lien under one of those," he answered.

Stephanie remarked, "Yesterday, there was an ungodly Trust of Kingship. We looked up the word and it does have to do with one's office. It would go under the ministry section in that list of Types of Trusts."[38]

We asked, "Are there other trusts?"

He replied, "Just like in life, there is an unfathomable amount of trusts for everything that Heaven has, every inheritance to the sons you can look at as a Godly trust. Satan, who is a copycat, wants to create ungodly trusts upon every Godly trust that Heaven has for us. Therefore, Wisdom is invoked, and Wisdom will tell you about an ungodly trust upon a Godly trust set for humankind."

Malcolm showed Stephanie an example from a session the previous day when Wisdom said, 'There is an ungodly trust against the trust of kingship which is someone's position."

He said, "Keep it simple, student."

Stephanie had the picture of someone peeling an onion and said, "The first part of the onion peeled back was the revelation of bonds."

She said, "He has asked me to ask you a question. 'How tedious did that seem at the time?'"

---

[38] See The Trust Registry in the Appendix

I replied, "Not overwhelming. We were just glad to have the revelation. It came unexpectedly, though. Of course, this has too."

Stephanie said, "Malcolm, keep me straight here please.

- Bring the tab forward (You will know there is an ungodly trust)
- Find the parameters around the ungodly trust
- Repent as necessary
- Strike the parameters
- Capture the princes—the dominion
- Freedom will come

"Well, that was simple. Thank you."

Stephanie remarked, "He just showed me, when you first start talking about consequential liens and bonds in your book, that this is at the very top of it. This is the step-by-step. It will be laid out correctly in the book, but it is a simple step-by-step. I am seeing 'K-I-S-S' big, too. It is a reminder to the people to *keep it simple, son*. This profound work *has* been made simple by the Father on behalf of the people because of His sovereignty and His love.

Stephanie was reminded of an occurrence in a session the day before where a kingpin was stripped of his regalia. Jesus was showing an enormous amount of love in the courtroom for that person and that even he is redeemable because of God's sovereignty and love. That is how firmly He is saying that this is His sovereignty and love for people; that is why He is going to make it simple. That is why He is giving this concept to the body.

With that, Malcolm leaned over and just kissed Stephanie on the cheek and walked out. She remarked, "That is the final kiss, keeping it simple. Thank you, Malcolm."

———·———

Chapter 17

The Treatise of Trust

Two Hebrew words are translated as trust in the Old Testament. The primary one is *bawtach*.[39] It means to find as a place of refuge. It carries a different level of strength than the other word *chasah*[40] (pronounced *kawshaw*). *Chasah* is more passive while *bawtach* stands boldly to say, "You can believe this!" It is *bawtach* that is used in Psalm 91 which has long been a favorite of believers. It is used in millions of prayers daily around the globe in daily devotions and seasons in the secret place. We have looked at it as promises of all sorts of protection, but we have never looked at it as a legal document between the Father and His Children. It is a form of trust providing benefits to everyone who calls on the name of the Lord.

> *And it shall be, that whosoever shall call on the name of the Lord shall be saved. (Acts 2:21)*

---

[39] H982—in Strong's Bible Concordance
[40] H2620—in Strong's Bible Concordance

A trust works like this. A trust contains provisions that, if the conditions are met, then you have the benefit of those provisions. If you don't meet the conditions, you are forfeiting the provisions.

Let's look at this Treatise of Trust containing promises and provision made to you and for you by the Lord Himself.

Psalms 91:1-16

[1] He who dwells in the secret place of the Most High shall abide under the shadow of the Almighty.

[2] I will say of the LORD, 'He is my refuge and my fortress; My God, in Him I will trust.'

[3] Surely, He shall deliver you from the snare of the fowler and from the perilous pestilence.

[4] He shall cover you with His feathers, And under His wings you shall take refuge; His truth shall be your shield and buckler.

[5] You shall not be afraid of the terror by night, Nor of the arrow that flies by day,

[6] Nor of the pestilence that walks in darkness, nor of the destruction that lays waste at noonday.

[7] A thousand may fall at your side, and ten thousand at your right hand; but it shall not come near you.

[8] Only with your eyes shall you look, and see the reward of the wicked.

⁹ Because you have made the LORD, who is my refuge, even the Most High, your dwelling place,

¹⁰ No evil shall befall you, nor shall any plague come near your dwelling;

¹¹ for He shall give His angels charge over you, to keep you in all your ways.

¹² In their hands they shall bear you up, lest you dash your foot against a stone.

¹³ You shall tread upon the lion and the cobra, the young lion and the serpent you shall trample underfoot.

¹⁴ Because he has set his love upon Me, therefore I will deliver him; I will set him on high, because he has known My name.

¹⁵ He shall call upon Me, and I will answer him; I will be with him in trouble; I will deliver him and honor him.

¹⁶ With long life I will satisfy him, and show him My salvation.

Now that you have read this passage, let's break it down to the component promises of this Treatise of Trust.

Psalms 91:1-16:

¹ He who dwells in the secret place of the Most High shall abide under the shadow of the Almighty.

The word *'trust.'* is also translated as a place of refuge, confidence, hope, make trust, or put trust (as in to put trust in).

The Father is qualifying who these promises belong to—those who dwell—abide—seek after intimacy with the Father, THEY shall abide under His shadow. The picture is of an eagle keeping her brood under the protection of her wings so no enemy can find them. They cannot be seen because they are under the shadow, covered by the wings of the Lord.

² I will say of the LORD, 'He is my refuge and my fortress; My God, in Him I will trust.'

Because of this provision of the Lord, this legal document of "Trust," you can confidently say that He is your place of refuge—where you abide so you can hide; however, that is not so much a defensive posture as simply a place of rest and safety. He is your God. You <u>can</u> <u>trust</u> Him! You can have confidence that what He says, He will do. If He has promised something, He can be relied on to fulfill it. He tells us that in Numbers 23:19, where it is written:

God is not a man, that He should lie,

Nor a son of man, that He should repent.

Has He said, and will He not do?

Or has He spoken, and will He not make it good?

You can have confidence in this detail of the Trust, for in Him it will come under the auspices of His Trust.

³ Surely, He shall deliver you from the snare of the fowler and from the perilous pestilence.

Another provision of this treatise is deliverance from the snare of the fowler and the pestilence that would seek to destroy you. A fowler sets nets and traps to entangle fowl as prey. You have a promise of protection from that.

The word for perilous implies an iniquity factor, so you have a promise of protection from plagues seeking to pass to you through your generational lines.

⁴ He shall cover you with His feathers, and under His wings you shall take refuge; His truth shall be your shield and buckler.

Again, the picture is of an eagle placing you in a secure place hidden from the eyes of those who would do you harm. The truth of what he has promised will defend you. A shield is primarily for frontal protection while a buckler is a surrounding form of protection. Picture a shield that encompasses you on every side.

> [5] *You shall not be afraid of the terror by night, nor of the arrow that flies by day,*

Because of the provisions of this trust made by the Father to you, you have absolutely no reason to fear attacks at night nor attacks by day. The protection of the Lord is complete.

> [6] *nor of the pestilence that walks in darkness, nor of the destruction that lays waste at noonday.*

Neither do you have to fear pestilence that travels in obscurity or is designed for wanton destruction. You also have the promise of protection from the destruction of any plague, including COVID-19!

> [7] *A thousand may fall at your side, and ten thousand at your right hand; but it shall not come near you.*

The promise extends to you regardless of its impact on those around you. The trust includes a promise of protection, whether from COVID-19 or any other plague cooked up in the courts of hell. We have a promise! Our Father can be depended upon.

⁸ Only with your eyes shall you look, and see the reward of the wicked.

We will observe the effects, but it is not our reward. If you are meeting the conditions of Psalm 91 by remaining securely in a place of intimacy with Father, you can remind Him of the provisions of this Treatise of Trust made between the Father and those who are His children.

⁹ Because you have made the LORD, who is my refuge, even the Most High, your dwelling place,

The Father did not stop at verse 8 with provisions of the trust; He goes on to enrich them in the next few verses.

¹⁰ No evil shall befall you, nor shall any plague come near your dwelling;

NO evil, not *some* evil, not *most* evil, shall be permitted to affect your household. The promise has been extended from you, to now include your household—your dwelling place.

Why is this so?

¹¹ for He shall give His angels charge over you, to keep you in all your ways.

The promise is for angelic protection that you can engage in your behalf. They will do what you cannot do. They can warn you and they can ward off attacks that you have no direct knowledge of. They will minister in your behalf to bring to bear the promises of this Trust. They will work to create a hedge of thorns about you for protection. They will attend to you. They stand ready and waiting for you to commission to them to fulfill all the promises of the Father for your life.

It is imperative that the Body of Christ learn to live offensively from the provisions of the Trusts of the Lord in our behalf, for far worse things are planned for our planet than COVID-19, as horrific as it has been. We must learn to stand in this place of insulation from the attacks on humanity and live from the secret place found in the realms of Heaven where we are co-seated with Him.

¹² In their hands they shall bear you up, lest you dash your foot against a stone.

The angels will help you stand firm without even the effects of injury to you as you continue your journey of sonship. Your angels need you to commission them to these tasks. They await activation of the sons of God to fulfill the promises of God on your behalf.

¹³ You shall tread upon the lion and the cobra, the young lion and the serpent you shall trample underfoot.

You have now passed from a passive stance and of one needing protection, to one where you have not only engaged your angels, but you are now standing in who you really are. You are a son, and it is time to begin to work offensively. You WILL tread, stomp, stand on the lion, AND the cobra, regardless of their size or age, you know your place!

¹⁴ Because he has set his love upon Me, therefore I will deliver him; I will set him on high, because he has known My name.

The Lord reinforces his promises and reassures His sons that He WILL deliver, He will set him in a high place—a place of dominion, simply because you have come to know His name. You know what His name represents. You know the implications of the many facets of His character. You are now understanding that He is your righteousness, your protector, your peace, you shield, your strength. He IS the Lord of the Hosts of Heaven, He is your provider, your healer, your banner of victory.

> [15] *He shall call upon Me, and I will answer him; I will be with him in trouble; I will deliver him and honor him.*

He promises that if you call—He will answer. He *will* be with you in times of trouble, He will deliver you, and He will honor you. He will hold you in a place of esteem. He will say of you, "This is My beloved son in whom I am well pleased!" That's you! It is not just someone else. It is you He has made this Trust agreement with. If you will *trust* Him, He will fulfill EVERY provision of EVERY promise He has ever made to you.

> [16] *With long life I will satisfy him, and show him My salvation.*

The final promises of the Trust of the Lord in this passage are two-fold—you will be satisfied, satiated, have enough of His kind of life here, that you are ready to transition to be in His presence in His realm, not this realm. Also, you will see His salvation, healing, deliverance, help, health, and welfare demonstrated throughout your life. You've seen the Trust of the Lord manifested in your life. It's time to go home now.

This passage is not the only Trust of the Lord recorded in Scripture. It is simply compiled into one passage in Psalms. We have mentioned Proverbs 3:5-6 and some others throughout this portion of the book. As you grow in understanding of your sonship, you will find yourself praying less from a defensive mode and morphing into a "this is who I am" mindset. The refrain from a song I have come to like says, "I am who I am because the I AM tells me who I am." It repeats that line over and over until it gets imbedded into your soul. Your spirit already knows the truth of that statement.

Another aspect of understanding I AM came from a definition Dr. Larry Lea (author of *Could You Not Tarry One Hour*) who defines I AM as "I will be who you need Me to be, when you need Me to be it."

If you need healing, He is Jehovah Rapha. If you need provision, He is for you Jehovah Jireh. Whatever the need, He is the provision for that need. No shortage exists, nor does any denial to His sons. Ladies, I am speaking of your position, not your gender, when I use the term *sons*.

We will look at a few more Trust of the Lord that will help us wrap our minds around what Heaven has done for us.

In Genesis we read where God was en*trust*ing Adam certain responsibilities following his creation. He said to him in Genesis 2:15-25:

> *15 Then the LORD God took the man and put him in the garden of Eden to tend and keep it. 16 And the LORD God commanded the man, saying, 'Of every tree of the garden you may freely eat; 17 but of the tree of the knowledge of good and evil you shall not eat, for in the day that you eat of it you shall surely die.' (you will be breaking the terms of the Trust and will be inviting calamity into your future!)* 41*

> *18 And the LORD God said, 'It is not good that man should be alone; I will make him a helper comparable to him.'*

> *19 Out of the ground the LORD God formed every beast of the field and every bird of the air, and brought them to Adam to see what he would call them. And whatever Adam called each living creature, that was its name. 20 So Adam gave names to all cattle, to the birds of the air, and to every beast of the field. But for Adam there was not found a helper comparable to him.*

---

41 My note.

> *²¹ And the LORD God caused a deep sleep to fall on Adam, and he slept; and He took one of his ribs, and closed up the flesh in its place. ²² Then the rib which the LORD God had taken from man He made into a woman, and He brought her to the man.*
>
> *²³ And Adam said: 'This is now bone of my bones and flesh of my flesh; she shall be called Woman, because she was taken out of Man.'*
>
> *²⁴ Therefore, a man shall leave his father and mother and be joined to his wife, and they shall become one flesh.*
>
> *²⁵ And they were both naked, the man and his wife, and were not ashamed.*

Adam had a great setup. He had plenty to eat, he had pleasant surroundings, he had regular communion with His Creator, and he was given companionship. His job was to fulfill his end of the trust agreement with the Father. Earlier in the same chapter we read:

> *⁷ And the LORD God formed man of the dust of the ground, and breathed into his nostrils the breath of life; and man became a living being (he became a being living in the original design of the Father). (Genesis 2:7-9)*

Paul describes our situation:

> *For in him **we live**, and **move**, and **have our being**; as certain also of your own poets have said, For **we are** also **his offspring**. (Acts 17:28)*

It is only in relationship to the Father that we actually live, that we are able to have *being*. Being comes from a word that means "I know why I exist!" We live out of the creators "I am-ness!"

> *⁸ The LORD God planted a garden eastward in Eden, and there He **put** the man whom He had formed.*
>
> *⁹ And out of the ground the LORD God made every tree grow that is pleasant to the sight and good for food. The tree of life was also in the midst of the garden, and the tree of the knowledge of good and evil.*

Adam was not created in the Garden of Eden; it was planted by the Father after Adam's creation and Adam was then put in the Garden. When He "put" Adam in the Garden it was an en*trust*ing it to him to tend it and keep it. "Put" was also translated as appointed, ordained, and ordered, among many other words. As Adam fulfilled his obligation to the Father, the obligations of the Father to Adam would be fulfilled in turn.

However, it wasn't long afterward that Satan came to interfere with this covenant/trust arrangement. His jealousy over the creation of God was demonstrated. He twisted the words that God had spoken to Adam to get him in a place of violation of the covenant arrangement Adam had. When God makes a covenant, He is creating a Trust—a legal agreement between parties.

Satan's sales pitch was that Adam and Eve would "be like God" knowing both good and evil. What Eve did not realize was that they already were like God, and they had an experiential knowledge of good, they just did not have an experiential knowledge of evil. They did not have to know evil in order to be well-rounded. Many have fallen for the sales pitch that you need to experiment with the world and what it offers in order to be well-rounded. That is a lie. It's as old as Adam and Eve in the garden. I don't have to taste the bad so I can appreciate the good. I can appreciate the good regardless.

The first things that happened to them was the realization of their vulnerability. They described it as being naked, but nakedness produces a state of vulnerability. It implies that people can see *ALL* of you. You have no secrets and no ability to keep things secret and guarded. The second thing was they tried to hide from God. Men have been hiding from God ever since.

Adam's disobedience resulted in his expulsion from the Garden of Eden and an immediate loss of the relationship with the Father that he had known. His original job description was to tend and keep the Garden of God in Eden. He lost his 'trust' and was fired from that position and from that point on, had to till the ground and work it to have produce to eat. Prior to that the garden readily produced without toil. It was work, but it was work without toil. The ease that the covenant/trust contained was gone. How we have longed for it to be restored.

Many have surmised from this encounter that God was mad at Adam and Eve. I think a better way to view it was he was disappointed in their disobedience just as you have experienced with your children when they did something you had instructed them not to do. We have lived with a fear that God was mad at us our entire lives.

You are His creation. You were made in His design. Substitute anger for disappointment and you will have a better comprehension of how the Father felt that day in the garden. Adam and Eve had to know consequences existed for their actions. The original design of the Father had been thwarted, but now, in Jesus, restoration of that design is possible. The *trust* had been broken. Now it needed to be repaired.

Many Scriptures are descriptions of the benefits of the Trusts instituted by the Lord in our behalf. To expound on these would take far longer than we have time to describe. As Holy Spirit leads, simply ask, "Is this another Trust of the Father in my behalf? or "Is it one of the benefits of the Trust of the Father?"

As Holy Spirit leads, study it out. I will include a list of several verses you will want to peruse concerning this in the next chapter.

——— · ———

Chapter 18
The Hall of Commerce

We are walking down a hallway. It reminds me of a corridor. It is not the usual place. Lydia was with us.

"Where are you taking us Lydia?" We asked. "The Halls of Commerce." We turned the corner, and it opened to a huge open room with a lot of people and a lot of activity in the room. It reminded us of a trading floor.

"Why are we here in the Halls of Commerce, Lydia?"

She replied, "Remarkable things are in store."

Stephanie explained, "She just showed me stores. Two words—like great things are in store for us, but also the word store, as in a place we would go to shop. This is the abundance of Heaven. This is the righteous trading floor of the peoples just like in the natural. Commerce you see and experience. There is a commerce in Heaven."

Lydia began instructing us, "One rightly dividing the truth. When you rightly divide the truth, when you understand the realities that Heaven is a trade and people rightly divide the truth about that, commerce is available—the commerce of Heaven which includes the goodness of God, the flow, the value, the frequency. Understanding and Wisdom trade here with the people on behalf of them. This is one of the great unknowns to most that there is value on the trading floors of Heaven. When people press in, when people choose to trade with Heaven, trade with the Father, trade with Wisdom and Understanding, there can be great exploits for the sons."

"Lydia, can you tell us how Heaven wants us to trade? Is this through tithes and offerings?"

She answered, "This is bigger and more than that.

Lydia said, "Do you see all the people here scurrying about—it is fast-paced. It is a fast-paced thing, like what you would see on the stock exchange floor in the natural, but it is much more organized. There is a lot of to and fro. I see what look like small offices around what would be the perimeter of this space. There is something in the middle that I need to focus on that they are coming to. I see the men and women in white linen going to it and then bringing those things to the offices around the edges of the Hall of Commerce."

Stephanie asked, "Can you explain that to me?"

Lydia instructed us, "It is a portal. It is where this trade happens in the hearts of people. This is a portal that is to the hearts and minds of you people. It is a decision. They are making a choice in and of themselves to trade the commerce of Heaven, the goods of Heaven, as sons.

"When they realize the true nature of being a son, all the goods of Heaven are accessible. This trading route is larger and bigger than most could comprehend. It is the favor of the Father, 'exceedingly, abundantly above what you could ask or think'[42].

"Think of it like this. There are goods and services in the earth realm that people see, seek out, and trade with. There are goods and services in Heaven. Remember types and shadows—that is what the earth is. It is a type and shadow of what the reality is in Heaven. As sons, you have full access of the Godly trades of Heaven."

Stephanie remarked, "Thank you, Lydia. This is interesting. I have never thought of it this way, where it is one portal. I only see it as one giant portal, but everyone can trade through that with their decision, their mindset, to trade on the trading floors of Heaven for goods and services of what Heaven brings into people's lives. Am I correct in my summation of this?"

"Yes," said Lydia excitedly as she leaned over, "but it is so much bigger than what you could think or imagine. That is what the Father wants people to know. He is so much bigger than what we could think or imagine. We

---

[42] Ephesians 3:20

can trade upon that thought process and that love that He has.

"No, we could not even imagine the things that He has for us, the things He is going to give us when we trade with Him—when we choose, and it is a choice."

Stephanie remarked, "She just said the phrase, 'goods and services,' like she is about to define it."

Lydia replied, "The goods of Heaven, the fruit of the Spirit, can be easily attained here. People have assumed that they are supposed to pull those fruits of the spirit out of themselves to trade here. It is what the Father brings to their hearts: goodness, kindness, gentleness, mercy, self-control. That is a good that can be given from this place."

Stephanie remarked, "I understand that, Lydia. What are services?"

Lydia answered, "What did Jesus do when He was on the earth? He served. The trades from here will cause people to want to desire what He did, which was to serve others. That is the truest form of love. The largest trade here is love. Love abounds in this place."

Stephanie commented, "I just saw people come out from the inside of that portal. Are you saying people can step into this place?"

Lydia replied, "They absolutely can. They can step into this portal, into this realm, into this gate, into this place, to trade the goods and services of Heaven into their own lives, which, in turn, has them trading into other people's lives as they serve them. Yes, a greater capacity is drawn from this well, from this place."

"That is really taking the load off us where we have had this mindset through religious thinking that we must stir this stuff up inside of us, that we must do these things in and of ourselves."

Stephanie then asked, "Are you saying that this is part of the goods and services of Heaven? That it is the gift? Is it those things coming from this place that allows us to be able to walk in the fruit of the Spirit and in serving others? It is like the pressure has been taken off us. Is that what I am seeing? Am I interpreting this accurately?"

Lydia said, "You see this correctly. This is the bestowing of these gifts from this place here—this trade route—this glorious trade route. Tell people they can step in this realm. They can step in through the gate. This gate was founded at the foundations of creation for people to freely walk, freely come here, freely receive. Truth abounds in love. This trading floor is where truth is found abounding in love—love for His people, love for His sons, and as sons, this is a place that you can come freely."

"Well, Lydia, this is a unique place." Stephanie observed. She then inquired, "How do people trade here?"

Lydia explained, "There are many in the body who feel they fail because they do not truly walk in the fruit of the Spirit. They cannot pull it out of themselves. They cannot walk in it the way that they want to walk in it. This is how they feel. This is how they perceive themselves. In this place, they can have the understanding that it is not them. It is Him. It is trading *with* Him as the goods and services of Heaven are for the sons of men. Have them step into this place. They will rejoice in the understanding that it is not in and of themselves, but it is the Father who brings these things out of them, through them, for others. The truest acts of service for others come from this place where love abounds.

"How can people think of themselves as failures when it is the Father that is bestowing these things in them and through them through this trade. It will take the pressure off people's hearts and minds that they must muster this in and of themselves. This is Him through them. This is what that means."

Stephanie remarked, "I like it. Lydia. It reminds me of how sometimes I tell the Father, 'Okay, Lord, this is what You said in Your Word, and this is how I believe. Now the ball is in Your court,' and it takes the pressure off my soul and my spirit to work anything out because He is doing it. That is what this place is, right?"

Immediately, Lydia took us back to the ballroom with all the balls—the safe place. In that ballroom we are serving others in a safe place. Then, a moment later we were back in the Hall of Commerce.

Stephanie said, "Thank you, Lydia, for showing us this. I am in awe of this room; it is massive. It is interesting to me, with these little, small offices around the perimeter how these men and women in white linen are coming from this trading floor portal. They are going in and out of it, and then going to these offices and getting the trades recorded."

I was reminded of Proverbs 4:7 that reads, "Wisdom is the principal thing; therefore, get wisdom. And in all your getting, get understanding." That is why Wisdom and Understanding are trades. They trade here with people.

I asked, "What would you choose?"

I replied, "I choose to access Wisdom. I choose to accept knowledge and that is the trade itself."

Lydia was beaming with joy.

We asked, "What question should we ask you next?"

Lydia replied, "Where do we go from here?"

We immediately found ourselves walking in through another door and down a hallway. We passed the Strategy Room and one of the angels waved as we went by. We walked past the Labor and Delivery Room. We went through an entry way into a giant basketball court.

Stephanie asked, "Is this a court (as in judicial) instead court (like in a basketball court)? What is this basketball court? I mean, that is what it looks like."

"There is a place of freedom that people need to really catch hold of things," Lydia responded.

Stephanie remarked, "When she said, 'catch hold of,' she threw the ball and I caught it. There have been a lot of references about balls lately."

Lydia continued, "Freedom is laying down old mindsets and precepts. Freedom is trading, nurturing, walking, and choosing this kingdom principle—that Heaven really is *this* close."

Stephanie said, "She just showed me walking up to a door and kicking the door open."

Lydia explained, "As people gain this knowledge and understanding of the concept of stepping into Heaven, not just stepping into the courts, but being in a place where there is freedom—freedom from the enemy, freedom from old mindsets and precepts. Laying it all down. That is what this is.

"You have heard of 'laying it all down' your whole life. When people choose to realize—they can step over the veil, step through the veil, that this access of freedom is for them—it will kick down the walls of old mindsets."

Stephanie remarked, "Like the feeling that you are showing me—we are on the edge of something so profound that people, many people, are going to lay their old mindsets down."

Lydia concluded, "It is going to kick down the doors and the walls for freedom for people. Keep pressing in as you do this work, as you say these things, as you tell the people how far the reverberation of this goes. More people are going to be drawn to this because they seek freedom. When they realize that they can trade with Heaven on this as easy as you have just been shown, the freedom is going to become tangible."

———·———

Chapter 19
Court of Trade

Stephanie commented, "I am watching an open basketball court and the phrase 'relaxing fun' is the only thing I can think of. What are you trying to show me? I am still seeing this basketball court. There is a trading court. As soon as I said that the whole room changed to a courtroom."

Stephanie remarked, "I just said in my mind, 'why didn't you just show me that from the beginning?'"

Lydia replied, "We are; we are teaching you how to pull things."

I asked, "Can you teach us about this?"

She replied, "Yes. This trading court is what is called the Court of Trades. It has a direct link to the Hall of Commerce. It has a direct link as if it is together."

Stephanie described, "I can see a swinging door with men and women in white coming in and out of this room from the Hall of Commerce into this Court of Trade, and

I am seeing men and women in white bringing paperwork to the Just Judge that is sitting at the Judge's Bench. He is signing papers and stamping things. Then these persons in white linen are going back out the door.

"The Just Judge turned and looked at us. We are about to see how this works here."

Expressing what she was observing, Stephanie explained, "I see the High Council and I see Jesus to the left. I am looking at the Judge's Bench. We are seated or standing behind them watching all of this and seeing a person in white linen coming from the right, bringing paperwork. There is a person (defendant) that is standing here with counsel. This is a person that is seeking a trade of goods and services with the Father.

"I see what is either an accuser or a prince, but this accuser is saying that the defendant cannot have full access of this trade because of generational sin and iniquity. Jesus is advocating on behalf of the person, that, because of what He did on the cross, that gives them free access to the trades and goods and services of Heaven.

The Father, the Just Judge, said to the person, "Are you choosing to seek a trade with the goods and services of Heaven?" This person said, "Yes," as an act of their will. Then the Just Judge asked, "Are you choosing to repent on behalf of your generations and to forgive them?"

The person said, "Yes." The accuser began presenting paperwork to the Just Judge who is looking at it. The accuser is saying that he is indebted with the trading floors of hell.

This is like in real time. The Judge is going over this paperwork and the accusers is to the side snickering. Jesus is not saying anything, because He has already said enough. The Judge looked at the enemy and said, "He is choosing to trade with Heaven, and I am overturning the trades with hell. Then He handed an eviction notice to the enemy. It said, 'Eviction Notice' on it.

Stephanie then noticed the accuser was wearing a crown. She reported, "It is a prince! This has to do with what we are learning about striking the parameters, the consequential liens, and the trust of trust with the Father. When we do this work of striking the parameters and getting the consequential liens overturned due to a person's act of the will to trade with Heaven and with the Father, it is because it is an open Heaven to the sons of men.

"This also serves as an eviction notice to the prince that is in people's hearts and minds. That is why they started out talking about trading of their hearts and minds.

"The prince was just served an eviction notice, and he is being taken out in chains. Now this person is given some paperwork, granting them open trade access, to open trade by trading with Heaven because of their choice, because they are choosing as an act of their will to trade with the Father, because this person sees himself as a son. Now, he is being let out of the courtroom, and there is another person that is here, and I am watching the same thing happen.

"What is interesting about this, is this person that I see, I see them with the full understanding of themselves, of who they are as a son. As an act of their will they are saying, 'I choose the realms of Heaven.' As an act of their will they are saying, 'I choose the reality. I choose to trade with Heaven.' I understand the reality that they cannot do this in and of themselves, and so their trading with Heaven is going to give them the fruit of the Spirit. It is going to give them full access to the goods and services, and this is one of the goods right here that we are watching play out—a dismantling of a prince in or upon their generations. That is why it is so important that this is an act of their will."

I commented, "Remember the Scripture, 'Choose you this day, whom you will serve'?"[43]

Stephanie remarked, "How I love the eviction notice. What is interesting is that the Father kept the legal paperwork from the enemy. He kept it. He did not give that back to the enemy. He gave him an eviction notice."

I asked, "What's happening with the second person?"

Stephanie responded, "This woman is making a declaration to the judge that 'I choose as an act of my will to no longer trade with the trading floors of hell, but as a son, I choose to trade in the Halls of Commerce with

---

[43] Joshua 24:15

Heaven.' Once she made that declaration, I am watching the Father. He took that paperwork that the enemy had given, and He shredded it and he handed that prince its eviction notice.

"The first thing that happens is the person is brought into the court. Jesus is to their left and a man or woman in white linen comes through the Halls of Commerce and hands the Just Judge the paperwork, which He reads. Jesus says, as an advocate on their behalf, what He has done at the cross. The enemy says that their generations did X, Y, and Z, and they have traded with hell. The Father takes the paperwork and tosses it. When that person says aloud that declaration, then the enemy is handed eviction papers.

"That is the process I am seeing over and over and over. Hallelujah Father!"

Stephanie began, "I say openly, we say openly, 'We, as an act of our will, we choose to trade with Heaven. We choose to trade with the Halls of Commerce to receive the goods and services from Heaven.'

"Immediately, I was standing in front of the Judge, and He was handing out an eviction notice.

"Thank you, Just judge! Thank you, Jesus!

"I just looked to my left. When I was standing in the back, Jesus was standing nearby. But when I looked to my left this time, He was wearing a crown and He said, 'My crown trumps that one every time!'"

Stephanie replied, "Yes, it does, Jesus!"

I asked, "How do people trade with hell?"

Immediately these thoughts came to Stephanie and me:

- Generational iniquities
- Choosing to do wickedness
- Celestial trades that are willful
- Literally making trades

Stephanie spoke what she was discerning, "Concerning the work we are doing with consequential liens, this is the last and final step. It is the final step. This is where we come to. That is exactly what this is.

"I just saw Kevin doing that prayer that we did recently on a Sunday and on a Tuesday when we sent the angels with the capture bags to capture the princes and then, the next step is we seek the eviction notice in the Court of Trades.

"We step into this court and as an act of a person's will, they make the statement:

> *As an act of my will, I choose and I forgive my family for trading with hell and as an act of my will and on behalf of my family, I choose to trade in the Halls of Commerce.*

———·———

Chapter 20
Becoming a Living Rainbow

Stephanie began our engagement with Heaven, saying, "Father, we praise your name and thank you for the truth of Heaven. We thank you that you have brought this revelation. We step into Heaven through Jesus' realm. Thank you for your help.

"We call our angels near, Ezekiel, his commanders, and ranks, and Wisdom. We are so excited you are here. We invite all the Seven Spirits of God, Council, Understanding, Knowledge.... Thank you so much, Heaven. We step in."

Stephanie asked, "What does Heaven have for us today? I call my spirit forward and tell my soul to sit down.

Describing what she saw, she said, "I am looking at a rainbow. We are outside with a beautiful hilly view, but there are mountains in front of me in the distance and I am looking at a rainbow."

"Hi Malcolm!" exclaimed Stephanie.

"Good morning," he greeted us, "Do you remember the promise?"

"I do, Malcolm, from Genesis," Stephanie announced.

He challenged, "Do you know that His promises are the same today?"

She replied, "I do Malcolm."

He said, "Look at the beauty of this landscape. It is like a landscape painting. Everything has its place. Everything is in its place. In this, you are looking at the promises of God—the inheritance that is for the sons."

Malcolm turned and faced me, declaring, "People can glean from these promises.

Think of the rainbow when you think of the revelation that is coming forth.

"Let it be a reminder—this landscape, this rainbow—that, as you are walking in this revelation, as it is becoming known, these are also the promises of God. They are just as evident as the rainbow has been, with the understanding of what God did in Genesis. His promises regarding these revelations are just as prominent, just as relevant, just as secure. The Father wants the people to know this. You learned yesterday about His love abounding through trades.

> *His love abounds in His promises to us, those that know and assume their sonship should fully see the rainbow.*

Stephanie expressed, "Malcolm, I see this rainbow, and I know that from Genesis when we see a rainbow in the natural, it is a reminder to us of that promise. As we are walking in this revelation, Malcolm, and we are expressing what Heaven is having to say about this, is there something you are saying in the natural, that we will know these promises? That we will see them as clear as we see the rainbow after a rain?"

We began walking toward the rainbow which was still large over the sky—over the landscape.

Malcolm assured us, "The promise is that this revelation is coming from the Throne of God, in that you can rest. The promise is more than just a natural rainbow that people will see. They will see this played out in their lives, and others will see the changes in them, the newness, the peace they will experience in and of themselves—a *living* rainbow of promises."

Stephanie acknowledged, "Malcolm, that excites me because people have said to me personally, that they have seen changes in my life and I can relate it to them now and say, 'You can view me as a living rainbow.'"

He responded, "Yes, the promise of God, instead of it being an actual rainbow in the sky, will be the living, breathing, walking promise of God of this revelation."

Malcolm picked up a couple of small rocks and began skipping rocks across the beautiful lake in front of us. He mentioned, "Skipping rocks is one of my favorite pastimes."

Stephanie stated, "I am enjoying the peace and the serenity this place."

He replied, "It is because you are a living, breathing testament of the rainbow. It has been your choice. Welcome."

Stephanie said, "You have talked to us for a couple of days in a row about this being a declaration of choice—to walk in the understanding and knowledge of the realms of Heaven, stepping through the veil of Jesus, having interactions in these dynamics of the Kingdom."

Malcolm declared, "This freedom, this place of freedom, this place of promise is for the sons.

---

*Be the living Testament
of the rainbow.*

"Walk in it. You will be amazed at those that are drawn to it. Father wants all his sons to enjoy this place. It is an inheritance that belongs to the sons. Seek it."

Stephanie explained to me, "As soon as Malcom said, 'Seek it.' I saw the verse, 'Seek first the Kingdom of God and His righteousness, and all these things will be added unto you.'[44] That is what this place is. All these things that are added unto us. This is part of that!"

Malcolm said, "Yes, people have been looking for an escape for an exceedingly long time. They find it in other things. They find it in other religions, meditation, occult practices. They find it in drugs and alcohol. *This* is what they are seeking. This is what the Father offers to the sons. This is a reprieve. This is a place to come. It is a true gift. Take it."

Stephanie replied, "Malcolm, we take it. I want to be a living Testament."

She noted, "Malcolm began walking down the hill and left me standing here."

"Hi Lydia!"

Lydia had just appeared so the two stood quietly admiring the scenery.

Stephanie asked, "Lydia, what questions do I need to ask you about this? Is this a display of Heaven for us to enjoy in the moment?"

She just turned and said, "Yes, that is what this place is. This is what the Father wants for His sons—a place of reprieve as they walk in their sonship—as they truly begin to understand who they are. This is what Heaven has to offer as an inheritance for them now. Not when

---

[44] Matthew 6:33

they come here when their bodies die, but it is for them—now!"

She then showed Stephanie a picture of the world as if she were in outer space, and she was looking at it with the turmoil that is in it.

Stephanie observed, "It was like there were two halves of the world and they were shifting back and forth, and the world was in great turmoil."

Lydia explained, "The turmoil upon the earth is increasing. The Father wants a place for His people to be able to land. This is what this is. Walk out your sonship; walk it out, and be the living testament of the promise. You have full access here."

Stephanie acknowledged, "Lydia, thank you for this. I do know many of us have understood that we can step in, participate, and be in the realms of Heaven; this is where we can find peace. It is where we can come before the Just Judge."

Lydia said, "Yes, but many do not realize that they are the product. As they walk in this, they are a part of it. It is tangible."

Stephanie explained to me, "Lydia just showed me people searching for the pot of gold at the end of the rainbow."

Lydia advised, "People will seek you out. They will be drawn to you."

Stephanie asked, "Is this related to the Halls of Commerce?"

"All of this is related," Lydia responded.

Stephanie remarked, "Now we are in that upper conference room, but through the window, I can still see the rainbow." She spoke to Ezekiel, who was present, "Hi Ezekiel! I see a lot of your ranks and commanders. I see my angel Citadel."

She noted, "He is large again in my presence," and asked, "Ezekiel, do you have something to say?"

He turned towards the window where she could still see the landscape with the rainbow outside the window, and he waved his hand across the window as if showing the panorama.

She said, "Ezekiel, I feel like it is a commissioning."

Ezekiel stated, "It is, it is a Bond of The Promise."

Stephanie said, "I see now it is a bond that we can request of the Father and commission the angels. The angels can bring to us the promise that allows us to be able to fully comprehend and move in this. The Scripture from Acts, 'In Him we live and move and have our being'[45] came to mind."

"That is what this bond will bring," Ezekiel declared.

---

[45] Acts 17:28

Stephanie remarked, "He is showing me the landscape and that the Bond of The Promise is like an instruction of ordered steps. It feels like it helps as we commission our angels to order our steps. This is part of that. It creates more of an ease of being able to walk as a living testament of the promise."

Ezekiel said, "As we release the Bond of the Promise upon those that do not understand this work, it also allows their spirit to be able to take a hold of this bond and begin to work it out in their lives. They will be drawn to those that walk in it and they will have the ability to walk it out on their own more easily. It creates an ease, but it is a bond."

Stephanie began,

Father, we ask for access into Court of Titles and Deeds, and we request on behalf of LifeSpring Ministries, and all of those that are drawn to it, all those that trade with it, all of those that work for it, and their families. We request the release of the Bond of The Promise with a writ of release of ease to the people. We commission Ezekiel, his commanders, and his ranks, and we commission our angels to go help deliver these bonds to the people, in the name of Jesus.

Ezekiel turned to me and spoke, "You have just made a trade." Then he winked and went away.

"This is why Heaven knows that the people need to hear this. I just saw a picture of me in prayer. Where there are days that it feels hard or you are going through something, to be able to step into this place; however, people see, hear, or sense, to see the rainbow and then take it upon themselves to be in that. Then ease comes as a reminder of all the promises that are here," Stephanie illustrated.

"Lydia, is there anything else that we need to know about this?" She had appeared in the room, but she was still leaning against the wall. Wisdom, Knowledge, and Understanding were also present.

Stephanie said, "Hi, Wisdom. Thank you for being here."

Wisdom said, "This is the wisdom of God, to impart peace amid turmoil. It is a reminder of His promises where many have lost hope. Many in the body have lost much hope. Father is in the reminding business. It is just a reminder. It is a reminder to the people of His promise. This place is His promise that we can be walking versions of that. This is just a reminder of that promise."

Stephanie concluded, "Thank you. Wisdom, Knowledge, and Understanding. I can see Ezekiel way in the distance, and I see the angels bringing this bond to people."

———·———

Chapter 21
Conclusion

The power and potential of this revelation can bring freedom to the sons on so many levels that it is hard to comprehend. In the few weeks that our Senior Advocates have been implementing these revelations we have seen major amounts of freedom in people's lives. People that had struggled for years with persistent challenges are finally free. The utilization of legal means provided by Heaven to result in freedom when properly applied is amazing.

We have seen dramatic transformation in people from the beginning of a Personal Advocacy Session to the end. The difference in their countenance was wonderful to behold. We have had testimony after testimony of the freedom experienced as we dealt with the ungodly trusts and the consequential liens affecting their lives.

The sad part of what we have seen concerning the ungodly trusts, is that many have had more trust in the power of the enemy to impact them than they have had in the love of the Father to come to their aid. They have been duped into believing in a devil and principalities who are defeated foes. As Malcolm so aptly reminded us "They are just a principality". They are defeated foes and we overcome them simply by repentance for us and our generations and by applying a few principles from the Courts of Heaven. Heaven made it simple, and we are so greatful that Heaven chose to share these insights with us, so that we could share them with you. I trust that you have been blessed, enriched, and challenged to overcome in every arena of your life as you have read this book, prayed prayers, and commissioned your angels to assist you. Let the capture bags work in your favor. Regain your innocence, so you can trust the Father again. He quietly waits for His sons to climb on his lap and spend time with Him.

We fully expect more revelation to be unveiled concerning the subjects of this book and as appropriate we will post them on our blog:

CourtsOfHeavenWebinars.com.

Be looking for them as it will be the simplest way to disseminate the new revelation.

May the contents of this book provide freedom for you and those you touch.

God bless you.

Appendix A

Extended Trusts Listing

Examples of Godly Trusts to Request

(Mostly Alphabetical)

Trust of Above and Beyond

Trust of Angelic Assistance

Trust of As if it Never Were (Spirit, Soul, and Body)

Trust of Boldness

Trust of Brotherhood

Trust of Clarity

Trust of Communion

Trust of Comfort of the Brethren, One to Another

Trust of Communion and Fellowship in the Holy Spirit

Trust of Courage and Confidence

Trust of Courage

Trust of Destiny

Trust of Deut. 11:24

Trust of Divine Health

Trust of Divine Health

Trust of Due Season

Trust of Divine Pathways to be Restored

Trust of Fairness and Equity   Trust of Financial Harvest

Trust of Father's Intent for Me   Trust of Forgiveness

Trust of Freedom   Trust of Friendship

Trust of Godly Portals on the Land

Trust of Harvest Returned for the Body of Christ

Trust of Honesty   Trust of Hope

Trust of In Time & Out of Time   Trust of Jesus' Blood

Trust of John 3:16   Trust of Knowledge

Trust of Love of Humankind   Trust of Loyalty

Trust of Luke 10:19   Trust of Mercy

Trust of Multiplication   Trust of My Scroll

Trust of One Race, One Blood   Trust of Passive Income

Trust of Passover   Trust of Prosperity

Trust of Precious in His Sight   Trust of Provision

Trust of Racial Harmony   Trust of Reconciliation

Trust of Redeemed   Trust of Redeemed Land

Trust of Relationships   Trust of Restoration

Trust of Restoration of Callings   Trust of Safety

Trust of Restoration of Lives   Trust of Salvation

Trust of Portals Restored to Their Original Purposes

Trust of Righteous Commerce   Trust of Self-Control

Trust of Sisterhood in Christ Trust of Sonship

Trust of the Glory of God Trust of the Supernatural

Trust of the Goodness of God Trust of the Word of God

Trust of Transfer of Ownership Trust of Trust

Trust of Unity Trust of Truth

Trust of Value Trust of Wholeness

Trust of Wisdom's Pearls

Ungodly Trusts to Remove

(Mostly Alphabetical)

- Trust of Abaddon (Death)
- Trust of Abortion
- Trust of Accusation
- Trust of Addiction
- Trust of Addictions—Alcohol, Drugs
- Trust of Alienation
- Trust of Anger
- Trust of Anxiety
- Trust of Astrology
- Trust of Auto-immune Disease
- Trust of Barriers
- Trust of Barriers of Darkness
- Trust of Bastard
- Trust of Bastard Curse
- Trust of Belial
- Trust of Betrayal
- Trust of Bewitchment
- Trust of Black Sheep
- Trust of Blasphemy
- Trust of Blocking of Breakthroughs
- Trust of Boisterous
- Trust of Blindness
- Trust of Bribery
- Trust of Broken Trust
- Trust of Brokenness (Marriages, Individuals' Lives)
- Trust of Calamity
- Trust of Can't Get Ahead
- Trust of Cancer
- Trust of Carousing
- Trust of Child Abuse
- Trust of Childhood Issues
- Trust of Chronic Sickness

Trust of Clashing Swords Over Marriages

Trust of Closed

Trust of Confusion

Trust of Crown of Dissension

Trust of Cultism

Trust of Curse Against the Family

Trust of Darkness

Trust of Death

Trust of Dementia

Trust of (Deception, Sorcery etc.)

Trust of Destruction

Trust of Dimed ("nickel and dimed") Paying attention to small amounts of money

Trust of Discord

Trust of Disturbed

Trust of Discouragement

Trust of Division

Trust of Doubt

Trust of Druidism

Trust of Embarrassment

Trust of Fallacy

Trust of False Gods

Trust of False worship

Trust of False, Evil Sacrifices

Trust of Falsehood

Trust of Family Curses

Trust of Favor Stolen

Trust of Fear

Trust of Financial Ruin

Trust of Financial Hardship

Trust of Freemasonry

Trust of Fruitless Efforts

Trust of Fright

Trust of Fruitless Efforts

Trust of Gluttony

Trust of Goat (Like Stool Pigeon, Sacrificial Lamb)

Trust of Hindered and Distressed

Trust of Hatred

Trust of Hindrance—Against Intimacy with Self, Others, Father God

Trust of Hindrance Against Honesty with Self, Others, Father God

Trust of Hindrance Against Openness

Trust of Hinduism

Trust of Idols

Trust of Human Wisdom

Trust of Incest

Trust of Ichabod (Glory Departed)

Trust of Instability

Trust of Inconsequential

Trust of Intellect

Trust of Injustices suffered

Trust of Lying

Trust of Isolation—Blockage of Access

Trust of Jealousy

Trust of Judas

Trust of Kindness & Peace Stolen

Trust of Knowledge

Trust of Lack of Fatherhood

Trust of Lies About Self

Trust of Lack of Provision

Trust of Livid (anger)

Trust of Loss of Fatherhood

Trust of Losses

Trust of Loss of Identity

Trust of Lying Tongues

Trust of Luciferianism

Trust of Lies

Trust of Lying Signs & Wonders

Trust of Mammon

Trust of Marine Spirits (Including Dagon-Fish god, Over One's Harvest, Sacrifice of Children

Trust of Marriage Curse

Trust of Mithraism

Trust of Mistrust (Those in Authority)

Trust of Mormonism · Trust of Mule

Trust of Murder

Trust of Myan/Incan/Aztec curse

Trust of Nomad—Bloodshed · Trust of Obstruction

Trust in One's Strength · Trust of Orphan

Trust of Orphanhood · Trust of Outcast

Trust of Owed · Trust of Poverty

Trust of Parkinson's Disease · Trust of Perversion

Trust of Pharmakeia · Trust of Pride

Trust of Polygamy (Concubines) · Trust of Racial Hatred

Trust of Praises Withheld · Trust of Racism

Trust of Premature Death · Trust of Rage

Trust of Profane Worship · Trust of Rape

Trust of Recurring Calamity · Trust of Ridicule

Trust of Repetitive Religious Behavior

Trust of Robbery · Trust of Secrecy

Trust of Seen · Trust of Self

Trust of Sexual Perversion · Trust of Sexual Trades

Trust of Shamanism · Trust of Shame

Trust of Shame and Blame · Trust of Sickness

Trust of Shame as a Father · Trust of Silenced

Trust of Shedding of Innocent Blood

Trust of Sickness & Disease
Trust of Siphoning
Trust of Slavery
Trust of Sorcery
Trust of Stagnation
Trust of Stolen Blessings
Trust of Stolen Destinies
Trust of Stolen Inheritances
Trust of Stool Pigeon
Trust of Stubbornness
Trust of Taking Money Under the Table
Trust of the Bastard
Trust of Trafficking
Trust of Trafficking of Children
Trust of Truth Denied
Trust of Ungodly Groups
Trust of Ungodly Religions
Trust of Ungodly Sacrifices
Trust of Ungodly Trades

Trust of Sin of Aladdin
Trust of Slavery
Trust of Soothsaying
Trust of Soul
Trust of Stealth Mode
Trust of Stolen Time
Trust of Stolen Virtue
Trust of Stonewalling
Trust of Strife
Trust of Taxation
Trust of Torture
Trust of Treachery
Trust of Unlovable
Trust of Walls
Trust of Witchcraft
Trust of Zodiac Signs
Trust of Zulu

The Trust Registry

- Trust of trust
- Trust as a father
- Trust as a son/daughter
- Trust as Income
  - Work
  - Stewardship
- Trust as a Friend
  - A friend that sticks closer than a brother
  - A friend to all
- Trust of Ministry
  - Trust of Platform
  - Trust of Prayer
  - Trust of Seed/Trust of the Word of God
  - Trust of Kings
- Trust of Family
  - Biological Family
  - Close Friends
  - Family of God

This is basically a Trust Registry and what we have been describing is your Personal page on your Trust Registry. But realize that because this is your Personal page, this Personal page affects all the other pages.

Step-by-Step Procedure

- Open the Bond Registry to the Personal page
- Bring the tab forward (You will know there is an ungodly trust)
- Find the parameters around the ungodly trust
- Repent as necessary
- Strike the parameters
- Capture the princes—the dominion
- Freedom will come

Capture Bag Colors & Their Meaning

Red—Infiltrations

Deep Purple—Something caught in a different time, age, or dimension

Black—Witchcraft/Sorcery/Luciferianism[46]/Satanism

Green—Plunder bags

Orange—Domains

Grey—Two-fold use: (1) Isolation and removal of ungodly frequencies, (2) Release of Godly frequencies and the frequency of Heaven

Brown—Land under evil dominion

Blue—Accusations

Pink—Innocence

Tan—Specific to domains of the enemy. Overlay them on treachery and heresy.

Gold—Glory bags

Silver—Essence & Love of the Father

---

[46] The worship of Lucifer. Freemasonry has this as their ultimate aim.

Multiplication[47]

by Amanda Winder

AmandaWinder.com

These blog posts are written by an amazing young woman who works with our ministry. She and her sister Bridget make a powerful team. As granddaughters of the late Healing Evangelist Dolores Winder, they share a wonderful legacy. Amanda recently shared these blog posts with our Platinum members. It is shared here as it is pertinent to what we are learning. Malcolm had connected this revelation to the chapter on The Trust Registry.

Last October, I shared about an evil timeline God cut me out of. I explained how my trading on the evil timeline caused me to receive a constant stream of

---

[47] https://amandawinder.ccm/2022/01/17/multiplication/

disappointment and perpetual woundedness in the realm of business.

After cutting me loose, Holy Spirit made it very clear that my angels had gone in and smoothed out the wrinkle in the timeline so that I could operate on the timeline Heaven ordained for me. He also said, "I am now going to be faithful and supply what you've trusted in another for. I am going to actually teach you how to do business from Heaven. You've waited so earnestly for this, constantly asking me for revelation."

Now, since that day, my life has changed in a significant way. I am able to connect to revelation concerning business that is revolutionizing my world.

Which is why I am here today. I am here to share about the principle of multiplication. Immediately after being cut loose, my angels and Holy Spirit started talking to me about trade and multiplication. He said, "The multiplication principle is the foundation of trade. It's how Lucifer fell so quickly. He started to multiply his seeds of iniquity. He began to create and design through trade. Of course, his creation was counterfeit, but he was multiplying with his trade. He used the fallen angels to help him with this.

"Amanda, multiplication comes down to seeds. A seed can multiply into a giant harvest that produces more seed. When Bridget gets a custom [art requests], that custom is a seed. That seed needs to be spoken to and over properly. That seed has the power within it to produce a larger harvest than that one custom. It can connect you to more people. It can connect you to more customs. It can literally open up so many trading routes in the Heavens. But you must speak that over it. You must sew multiplication into it. You must treat it as a blessing. It must be treated as a newly established trade route, with a future purpose.

And you aren't just establishing trade routes with a seed of multiplication, you are also opening realms, dimensions, portals, and timelines.

So, when you produce a new writing, see it as a seed. Take that seed in your spirit's hands and follow these instructions:

- Study the content of the seed. If it is a writing, ask Me what My intent is for it. How do I want to reach people through the words you are speaking? If it is a custom or something else your sister is creating, again, ask Me about it. Ask Me what My intentions are for it. How can that piece of art hanging in someone's home edify the space? How can a *Singing-and-Painting* split through the current frequency waves and open up more of Heaven in the space or place of the person viewing it?
- Then, coat the seed in gold for ultimate and eternal protection.
- Next, establish and open up bridges, tunnels, pathways and lines of communication and connection. They will kind of look like roots in

the spirit. Open ended, but entitled and prepared for more growth as they connect to others.
- Very important step! Encode the seed with the principle of division, so that it will divide the works of Satan and the kingdom of darkness or the defeated kingdom.
- Next, assign and commission cherub angels to each seed (they love this work) to water the seed and help it grow to fruition.
- And last, but honestly the most important component, plant the seed in the realms of God. Planting them in My realms ensures that the seeds will overflow from My throne on high. They will be an outpour from the highest heights with a direction to come down low into the second heaven and then the earth realm so that they may begin to do a new work in creation.

Here are the names/realms of God I currently use:

Jehovah-Jireh—God Our Provider (Genesis 22:12-14)

Jehovah-Rapha—God our Healer (Exodus 15:22-26)

Jehovah-Shammah—God who is There (Ezekiel 48:30-35)

Jehovah-Nissi—God our banner of victory (Exodus 17:15-16)

Jehovah-Tsidkenu—God is our Righteousness (Jeremiah 23:6)

Jehovah-Hoseenu—God our Maker (Psalm 95:6)

Jehovah-Makedesh—God our Sanctifier (Leviticus 20:8)

Jehovah-Rohi—God Our Shepherd (Psalm 23:1)

Jehovah-Shalom—God our Peace (Judges 6:24)

Jehovah-Gibbor—God who is Mighty (Psalm 24:8)

Jehovah-Izzuwz—God who is Strong (Psalm 24:8)

Jehovah-Elohim—God who is Creator (Genesis 2:4)

Jehovah-Sabaoth—God of the Hosts of Heaven (Isaiah 14:27)

Now, remember, whatever you're doing from Heaven is large and powerful. It's linked to your human spirit, which is designed to operate from a place of kingship as it governs over the heavens and the earth. Also, this principle is weighty because it contains My glory. You are trading with My glory for the kingdom's sake."

In this moment, I have been using the principle of multiplication for 3 months. George (my chief personal angel) instructed me to use it as much as possible. Holy Spirit also told me to make a list of where I use it and how I use it. Now, I'm not the best at keeping up with how I use this principle because I often find myself using it in the moment; however, I do keep a record in my journal every day because I see the literal day as a seed. I see the day as a seed of multiplication that has the potential to expand and multiply from the realms of God.

———·———

Multiplication, Part II[48]

by Amanda Winder

AmandaWinder.com

After I shared the blog about multiplication on Monday, I woke up on Tuesday and began asking Holy Spirit about the principle. I felt deep in my spirit that there was more He wanted to share with me because questions about the principle began to fill my mind and heart.

So, I sat down with Heaven on Tuesday morning and started asking questions. G (George, my chief angel) came forward and said, "Now, the truth of the matter is there is so much more to explore with multiplication. You've merely just scratched the surface of it. You see the seeds you are planting can actually become full-functioning trees of life. But they must be continuously watered. They need care to grow." I said, "Can the KOD (kingdom of darkness) steal the seeds planted in the realms of God?" G said, "They can't necessarily steal

---

[48] https://amandawinder.com/2022/01/20/multiplication-part-ii/

them the way in which you are thinking. Jehovah's power is all consuming. Demons and fallen angels can't just waltz up to a realm and steal the seeds; however, they can be given access. They can be given access in many ways. There are many openings that can provide a pathway for the seeds to be stolen." I said, "What does the KOD do with a stolen seed?" G said, "Well they will try to take it apart and dismantle it for parts. They are looking to see how the principle of division can dismantle their works; however, they are prevented entry into the seed because it is coated in gold for protection purposes. Something you might do is actually give the seed a key. Create a lock and key for the seed. A lock and key that can only be used for entry and exit purposes by you (the designer) or Heaven. Assign an angel to take the key and store it in a lockbox in Heaven. Mark it 'Seed Keys.' The angel will keep track of each seed key and each lock that a seed is using."

Then I asked, "What about demons that can pick a lock?" George said, "Good question. Those types of demons do exist. They use their ancient minds and corrupted wisdom from Heaven to open locks. So, then you would need to assign the cherub angel with an extra role. They need to be assigned to keep lock-picking demons away. And if they need reinforcement, they need to be given the ability to call for the reinforcement" I said, "Well…could we maybe use a frequency sound instead? A sound that chases or warrants pick-pocketing demons away?" G said, "Yes! Yes, you can absolutely do that. It might honestly be easier to do something of that nature. So, tell the seed to vibrate with the energy from the Father's throne. That energy is light, and the light is a powerful frequency, keeping pick-pocketing demons away."

I then said, "I want to know about the consumer of the seeds' interaction. Can they harm the seed and its growth?" G said, "Yes, yes they absolutely can. But it's different than what you are thinking. A consumer harms the seed by not receiving it properly. But that's not on you or your works. That is within the consumer's heart alone. It's not for you to worry about, honestly, because the seed will continue to be a gift of frequency and growth in that person's life. The Father will continue to pursue the person's heart until he/she is operating where the Father needs him/her."

Marvelous right? It's all so marvelous to me that I implored Heaven about it again today. G said, "The completeness of multiplication is found in this... After much practice with the principle (your spirit knows it well), your soul will have an understanding, and then you won't have to continue to repeat the steps. The purpose of repeating the steps over and over again is to give your soul a lesson in understanding how this principle works. I don't want your soul doubting what you're doing.

"Amanda, doubt will immediately stop the flow of multiplication. It will cause the roots from the pathways of connection to shrivel up. They will stop expanding if doubt gets in the way. And it's because you will have sewn the intent of doubt inside of the seed. Which is why it is so important that your intent of the seed is from the Father's heart. You must have your spirit man forward and your heart prepared to link to the Father's when you are sowing a seed. Keep malice and destruction out. Keep doubt, fear, unbelief, and confusion out. Keep the soul out of the sowing of the seed.

"Remember what you were told about cultivation being a principle of identity and multiplication being a principle of kingship?"

Then George stopped and told me to go back and read through those notes.

In the notes, Father said this, "Amanda, seeds come down to intent. So, it is imperative that you have a developed relationship with your human spirit and Holy Spirit before you use the principle of multiplication. Multiplication is a duty. It's a working duty from a place and position of royalty in the Heavens.

"You see, cultivation is more of a principle of identity. You are coming into the kingdom and into relationship with all of creation... All of creation. You're establishing something deep within the recesses of life when you cultivate. Deeper cultivation opens up avenues for deeper relationship and connection to identity. Identity is foundational. It's imperative that you have a solid and firm foundation of who you are as a daughter or a son in My kingdom.

"Then comes kingship. Then comes royalty. A prince doesn't know he's a prince at infancy. He must come into that knowledge and understanding as he develops, grows, and matures in the kingdom he has been born into. And it's okay. It's okay that he doesn't understand who he is yet. It's not needed for him to understand yet. Yes, he might know he is different, but the level of understanding must be developed with time. The same is true with Me and My kingdom. If people can simply grasp who they are from Heaven's point of view first... If they can cultivate first, then they can become multipliers as they govern in accordance with their role of kingship. Which requires acceptance and then a cultivated relationship with one's power, dominion, and authority. How can one operate in multiplication if one does not understand of the power, dominion, and authority one possesses?"

———·———

Division

by Amanda Winder

AmandaWinder.com

About a month ago, I was speaking with one of my angels. I saw him walking in the distance from a field. He came closer with a scroll. He said, "I have the scroll, but this part needs to be unlocked." Then I saw another tiny scroll inside of the larger one, but it was locked. Now, the angel had the key he needed to unlock the scroll (I gave him a few days before); however, he needed my lead to unlock it. So, with my commission, he unlocked the tiny scroll inside. The scroll began to unroll. It rolled and rolled and rolled. I said, "It's longer than the large scroll." Topucca, the angel replied, "Yes longer, but secret knowledge is contained inside."

So, what did the tiny scroll contain?

"The old ways of receiving and knowing Jesus are in the past. We are in a new paradigm where who He is will

---

[49] https://amandawinder.com/2021/12/14/division/

be presented very differently. But it will be a whole and complete way and method.

"Jesus is so many things. People have been deeply distracted from this truth because of religion's desire to suffocate the truth. The more Jesus is suppressed, the less people know the Father, His heart, and the realm of Heaven in its fullness. Remember, Satan's goal is to always oppose the Father, drawing people deeper into darkness and pain.

"Most humans see themselves as flawed, broken, and deeply wounded. And they are. Don't get me wrong. Humanity is flawed, fractured, and broken; however, and there's more... There's a deeper truth that draws humans in, which is that they can... You can be divided from that brokenness. God can separate the dark from the light. He sees His children in right standing through Jesus, and He wants to pull you into a deeper measure and fullness of His light and His love.

"Humans think of division as an evil thing because of the current culture. But there is a basic meaning to it. To split in two. To sever. To cut in half. It's not an evil thing. Satan, in his corruption, has used division for evil purposes. Just like he has twisted light for his own gain.

"Division is a word that isn't used in the current believing culture. But it's a word that I would have you use as an ecclesia, as a body of governing believers over the heavens and the earth. I would have you use the word divide."

Fascinating right?! God is a divider. He's in the business of division. He is in the business of splitting us from the evil, darkness, and iniquity that dwells in us, through us, and within our realm of life.

Just the image of it. Just the language itself. It's powerful. Like Topucca said to me, "It's very, very piercing. This word carries weight, and it travels quickly throughout the ethosphere. It's taps deeply on the foundational essence of humanity."

Truly, it contains much more than my soul can comprehend. I've needed my human spirit to grasp this truth and cultivate a lifestyle of it over the past month.

Now, you might be wondering, "How are you cultivating a lifestyle of division?" Well, I followed Holy Spirit's lead when Topucca said this, "That's all vulnerability is Amanda. It's the expression of evil, darkness, pain, and iniquity. Truth (no matter what it is) gains its power when darkness is brought out into the light. As soon as it's spoken from a place of rawness, intimacy, and vulnerability, the light captures the darkness and begins its process of division."

So, division is where I've been resting. I've begun to rest on the truth that God is always in the business of dividing us from evil and darkness with light, and that light is Jesus. Jesus isn't a man in a story book. He isn't the hype that religions argue about. Instead, He is a very real and alive. He dwells in realms and dimensions we cannot see with our physical eyes, but must see and experience through the eyes of our activated human spirits.

And He is wanting to divide us from the darkness and pain we are currently experiencing, but we must become vulnerable enough to express it. We must not be afraid to share the deepest measure of our hearts, no matter what it might look like. Because, once we do... Once we've shared the darkness lurking around inside of us and the realm that surrounds us, then God has the opportunity to split us from the darkness with His light... Bringing more life, love, and peace than we've ever experienced before.

———·———

Scriptures of Trusts

Ruth 2:12 "The LORD repay your work, and **a full reward be given you by the LORD God of Israel**, under whose wings you have come for refuge."

2 Samuel 22:3 "The God of my strength, in whom I will trust; **My shield** and **the horn of my salvation, My stronghold** and **my refuge; My Savior, You save me from violence.**"

2 Samuel 22:31 "As for God, His way is perfect; the word of the LORD is proven; **He is a shield to all who trust in Him.**"

Psalm 2:12 "Kiss the Son, lest He be angry, and you perish in the way, when His wrath is kindled but a little. **Blessed are all those who put their trust in Him.**"

Psalm 5:11 "But let all those rejoice who put their trust in You; let them ever shout for joy, because **You defend them**; let those also who love Your name be joyful in You."

Psalm 7:1 "O LORD my God, in You I put my trust; **save me from all those who persecute me; and deliver me,**"

Psalm 16:1 "**Preserve me**, O God, for in You I put my trust."

Psalm 17:7 "Show Your marvelous lovingkindness by Your right hand, O **You who save those who trust in You From those who rise up against them.**"

Psalm 18:2 "The LORD is **my rock** and **my fortress** and **my deliverer**; My God, **my strength**, in whom I will trust; **My shield** and **the horn of my salvation, my stronghold.**"

Psalm 18:30 "As for God, His way is perfect; the word of the LORD is proven; **He is a shield to all who trust in Him.**"

Psalm 25:2 "**0 Keep my soul**, and **deliver me; Let me not be ashamed**, for I put my trust in You."

Psalm 31:1 "In You, O LORD, I put my trust; **let me never be ashamed; deliver me in Your righteousness.**"

Psalm 34:8 "Oh, taste and see that the LORD is good; **Blessed is the man who trusts in Him!**"

Psalm 34:22 "The LORD **redeems the soul of His servants, and none of those who trust in Him shall be condemned.**"

Psalm 37:40 "And the LORD **shall help them** and **deliver them;** He shall **deliver them from the wicked**, and **save them**, because they trust in Him."

Psalm 57:1 "Be merciful to me, O God, be merciful to me! For my soul trusts in You; and in the shadow of Your wings I will make my refuge, **until these calamities have passed by.**"

Psalm 64:10 "The righteous **shall be glad** in the LORD, and trust in Him. And **all the upright in heart shall glory.**"

Psalm 71:1 "In You, O LORD, I put my trust; **let me never be put to shame.**"

Psalm 141:8 "But my eyes are upon You, O GOD the Lord; in You I take refuge; **do not leave my soul destitute.**"

Psalm 144:2 "**My lovingkindness** and **my fortress, My high tower** and **my deliverer, My shield** and **the One in whom I take refuge**, who subdues my people under me."

Proverbs 30:5 "Every word of God is pure; **He is a shield** to those who put their trust in Him."

Isaiah 57:13 "When you cry out, let your collection of idols deliver you. But the wind will carry them all away, a breath will take them. But he who puts his trust in Me **shall possess the land,** and **shall inherit My holy mountain.**"

Works Cited

American Heritage Dictionary of the English Language, Fifth Edition. Houghton Mifflin Harcourt Publishing Company, 2016.

Description

Are you living from storm to storm with seemingly no relief? Heaven has solutions that are unpacked in this book. As we understand the concept of heavenly trusts and consequential liens, we will enter new phases of freedom that we have never experienced before.

These concepts aren't new, they are simply new to us. Dig in and find out how to live as the son or daughter of God you were meant to be, free from the plague of constant storms and being tossed to and fro. You were built for more than that. Begin to experience it today!

About the Author

Dr. Ron Horner is an apostolic teacher specializing in the Courts of Heaven. He has written over twenty books on the Courts of Heaven, Engaging Heaven, working with angels, or living from revelation.

He currently trains people in engaging the Courts of Heaven in a weekly online teaching session. You can register to participate and discover more about the Courts of Heaven prayer paradigm through his various websites, classes, products, and services found here:

www.ronhorner.com

Other Books by Dr. Ron M. Horner

Building Your Business from Heaven Down

Building Your Business from Heaven Down 2.0

Cooperating with The Glory

Courts of Heaven Process Charts

Dealing with Trusts, & Consequential Liens

Engaging Angels in the Realms of Heaven

Engaging Heaven for Revelation – Volume 1

Engaging the Courts for Ownership & Order

Engaging the Courts for Your City (*Paperback, Leader's Guide & Workbook*)

Engaging the Courts of Healing & the Healing Garden

Engaging the Courts of Heaven

Engaging the Help Desk of the Courts of Heaven

Engaging the Mercy Court of Heaven

Four Keys to Dismantling Accusations

Freedom from Mithraism

Let's Get it Right!

Lingering Human Spirits

Living Spirit Forward

Overcoming the False Verdicts of Freemasonry

Overcoming Verdicts from the Courts of Hell

Releasing Bonds from the Courts of Heaven

Unlocking Spiritual Seeing

SPANISH

Cómo Proceder en la Corte Celestial de Misericordia

Las Cuatro Llaves para Anular las Acusaciones

Liberando Bonos en las Cortes Celestiales

Liberando Su Visión Espiritual

Sea Libre del Mitraísmo - Segunda edición

Tablas de Proceso de la Cortes del Cielo

Viviendo desde el Espíritu

www.ingramcontent.com/pod-product-compliance
Lightning Source LLC
Chambersburg PA
CBHW022003160426
43197CB00007B/251